The

FACES

behind the pages that

INSPIRE

"Lori Rekowski has done it again! . . . She has assembled a rich assort-
ment of co-authors and given us a blessed peek into these seekers' lives
of how to aim higher in life. . . . What a collection for lifting the spirit
and touching the soul – a must read – thank you Lori."
—Patricia Ogilvie, *www.patriciaogilvie.com*

"If you find yourself feeling a tad cynical about what's going on in your
life or in the world at large, do yourself a favor. Curl up with this book
for a few hours. The worst that will happen is that you'll find some
hope slipping back into your awareness. But be careful, they just might
inspire you to want to take the next step and become 'one of them.'"
—K.J. Allen

The
FACES

behind the pages that

INSPIRE

Keller —
You are such
an incredible
Light!!
Enjoy life —
Lori

LORI REKOWSKI
and
FRIENDS

Internet addresses given in this book were accurate
at the time it went to press.

Author Lori Rekowski is available as a speaker and consultant. Please visit
www.facesbehindthepagesthatinspire.com for her schedule of appearances.

Cover and Interior design by Frame25 Productions
www.frame25productions.com
Cover art © ra2 studio c/o Shutterstock.com (computer and hand image)
Yuri Arcurs c/o Shutterstock.com (faces montage)

Library of Congress Cataloging-in-Publication Data

Rekowski, Lori, 1962-
The Faces Behind the Pages That Inspire/Lori Rekowski & Friends
Includes bibliographical references.

ISBN 978-1-478388-73-9

One faces the future with one's past.
—Pearl S. Buck

I dedicate this book to Mark Zuckerberg

For without his gift of vision and passion,
millions of people around the world
would not have found a place of refuge — in this special place
he named Facebook — and countless souls would be
without the doses of hope, humor, inspiration, and
compassion that we deliver to our extended community
of "friends" through our Pages.

Contents

A Personal Note From Lori Rekowski

Experience is not what happens to a man,
it is what a man does with what happens to him.
—Aldous Huxley

I AM AN INTUITIVE. I often receive "visions" (pictures that flash in my mind) of things to come, and the birth of this book was no exception. I happened to be on a phone call with a remarkable woman, Karen Mayfield, of *Wake Up Women*, discussing an upcoming world tour that we were going to collaborate on...when the vision of this book "showed up" in my mind. When I receive visions *that* clear, I pay attention — and I do my best to follow the guidance that I receive along with them. And, this book project is no exception.

For years, I've done my best to listen, meditate, pray and ask for guidance that would allow me to do work to help heal others in a way that is for the highest good of all concerned. In the process of practicing this, I find that I am always blessed. This project has been no exception.

Seriously, I cannot begin to share with you how fascinating the journey has been in creating this book. Although, at times, the process has been exhausting, I am simply awed by the fact that I have had this opportunity to work side by side with some of the most warm, caring, loving, talented and respectful people on the planet today. If you think that I am laying this on "a bit thick," then I challenge you come back to this note after you've read the book and revisit your initial judgment of my claims.

My co-authors in this book are about as authentic as human beings come. I've learned that they truly do love and care about their fans and subscribers, on a level that only truly special and very gifted human beings can. And, each of them has a heart as big as they come. They are sincere, thoughtful, compassionate and so passionate about helping people — by sharing what it took for them to want to help others in the pages to come — that I am truly humbled to be in their presence.

Combined, they have gone through some of the most difficult life challenges that anyone could ever face: one of our authors experienced what I consider to be the worst possible thing that a parent could go through, losing a child; another experienced her husband being murdered and — equally and incredibly sad — she was kidnapped, raped, and held captive and tortured for five days before escaping.

And, frankly, *every single one of their stories* is fascinating and compelling — and in the end, they are an example of the remarkable resilience that each of us, as human beings, have, residing within us.

When I received a similar vision to write my first book, *A Victim No More*, I realized quickly that my life would never be the same. Believe me, that was an understatement. I had "miracle after miracle" occur on my journey to this moment in time. And, almost every single thing that was "shown to me in that vision" has come true. I have a feeling that the final "segment" in that series of three insights/visions that I received more than ten years ago, is about to happen here with this book.

Now, not long after the second edition of my book, *A Victim No More, How to Break Free From Self-Judgment,* was published in 2006 by Hampton Roads Publishing Company, my life began to unravel. It seemed that every single thing that I wrote about in that book would be tested through more personal life challenges. I thought that, as a woman, I'd pretty much have gone through everything a woman could go through in a tragic life lived in the victim mindset. Well, I was dead wrong. There was more ahead.

While I am not going into *that* story in this book, I will say that what I haven't gone through in life challenges and tragedies personally, my co-authors in this book have.

In March 2008, I sustained a brain and neck injury that sent me into four long years of a man-made hell. I no longer take one single day of my life for granted. The beauty of this story is that because I chose to practice what I taught in my previous books, I now have the great honor of still proclaiming "I am not a victim anymore."

And, better yet, I have found other like-minded individuals with whom I can share my journey. I am now stronger, more determined and blessed beyond boundaries to be able to say that I have 32 fellow authors who can boldly state, *by their own life examples*, that they are free from the victim mindset, as well. They are celebrating their lives as courageous *victors*, committed and poised to continue to "pay it forward" through their respective fields of work — and dedicated to inspiring all of us in the social media world of Facebook.

With love and respect,

Lori Rekowski

Introduction

The person who tries to live alone will not succeed as a human being. His heart withers if it does not answer another heart. His mind shrinks away if he hears only the echoes of his own thoughts and finds no other inspiration.
—Pearl S. Buck

MILLIONS OF SUBSCRIBERS FLOCK to their computers each and every day to find community and support within the Facebook network. Many of those subscribers have found tremendous hope when they had felt none — within the interface of this special space created by a young genius, Mark Zuckerberg.

Due to the generosity of some very special people that you are about to meet, many have found the safe "space" of refuge and relief that they once longed for. In Facebook terminology, they are called Page (Admins) Administrators.

Who are these driving forces behind the scenes who find themselves dedicated, day in and day out — passionate about their causes — and to serving and encouraging their *followers* tirelessly? Now, you can meet them here in the pages of this remarkable book.

This book will reveal their very personal victim-to-victor stories to you. These heart-warming and inspiring life stories will take you on a journey of hope, wonder, fascination and encouragement.

Hi, my name is Lori Rekowski. I am an author and business entrepreneur. A mother. A grandmother. And, I am a very curious person. I am always eager to learn. And, sometimes, I am even nosey! Like many of you, I joined Facebook to connect with friends and family. My daughter told me that I needed to "get with it, get with the times and check Facebook out, Mom."

I jumped aboard the fast-moving train of social media and gave it a try. Much to my surprise, I became enthralled. I found myself spending more and more time seeing what this "place in cyberspace" had to offer.

At first, I simply connected with friends and family—and had a blast doing so. I was keeping in contact with my nieces, nephews, high school friends and relatives that I hadn't been in touch with for years.

And then, I discovered Café World, Farmville, and other fun games that, honestly, I frankly almost felt addicted to. It was a blast. In time, I began to tire of some of those games, and I found myself hungry to explore more of what Facebook had to offer. *And then, it happened.* A friend of mine shared a post that seemed to be "speaking to me."

It was a beautiful picture with an embedded message, featuring a quote from a famous person. This particular message spoke to me in a way that meant a whole lot — especially on that particular day — when life had me a little down. I related deeply to what it said, and it encouraged me on a day when I really needed it!

Friends began sharing more and more of these posts, and then one day, I clicked on the source of one of the pictures and discovered an entire Page filled with these wonderful inspirational messages!

That was it. I was hooked. I had discovered a Fan Page. And frankly, it changed my whole experience of Facebook. I was loving it — so much so, that I decided to start one of my own!

Being the curious person that I am, and having extra time on my hands, one particular day I began to wonder who these people *were* behind the scenes of my daily inspiration. And then I asked myself the question: Why do they devote their time so freely to inspire others? This admin stuff was a whole lot of work for me; I knew, firsthand, how much time it took to create my Page!

It didn't take long before I realized that all of our time was donated. No one was paying a dime for these fabulous messages. And so, my curiosity got the best of me.

I wanted to know why these people gave so freely of their time to build these amazing communities — communities that I noticed had been growing for years already! Day in and day out, I observed how they spent their valuable time to inspire, inform and interact with us.

So I set out to discover who these mysterious people really were.

Here's what I found:

Behind the scenes of your Facebook experience are doctors, nurses, attorneys and Ph.D.s in a myriad of fields. There are professional athletes, professional coaches, social workers, professors, psychics and experts in more fields than I have time to list here.

With the simple click of your mouse, you can subscribe to Pages maintained by Page Administrators who have qualifications that many people pay thousands of dollars a year to access in their hometowns.

And I found that most of my fellow subscribers had no idea who these dedicated (and most often) anonymous people behind the scenes were! These were our "Admins," women and men who are tirelessly creating the posts day in and day out — posts, my friends, that "feed our minds" with inspiration, information and so much more!

As I mentioned in my personal note to this book, I authored a self-help book entitled *A Victim No More, How to Stop Being Taken Advantage Of.* I had set up a Facebook page myself to let people know that my book was still available. Funny, I hadn't done much with my page. Then, the "A Ha" moment came: Why don't I start posting some inspirational messages based on what I taught in my book? And so, the lessons began.

I also began exploring other inspirational Pages where I could share amazing posts. I found many fabulous and unique Pages along the way. I learned that I was not alone in wanting to discover who these people were "behind the scenes." So, I set out to find an eclectic group of Page Admins and get their stories.

Now, I was fortunate. They let me in to their worlds graciously. And because of their generosity, you can join me, too, in discovering their fascinating and inspiring stories about why they actually do this tireless work on our behalf.

Come join me. You've now got a "back stage pass."

*We only have to look around us to see how
complexity and psychic temperature are still rising:
and rising no longer on the scale of the individual
but now on that of the planet.*
—Pierre Teilhard de Chardin

Meet Tim Miejan of *The Edge:*
Soul of the Cities

Getting to the Heart of it all
by Tim Miejan

LET ME INTERJECT A BRIEF note here, before I start, about my relationship with this book.

I met Lori Rekowski, this book's creator, some time ago in the Twin Cities. She was an entrepreneur working on her first book, A Victim No More, and I was managing editor of The Edge, a free, monthly holistic publication that has served the Upper Midwest since 1992. Lori approached me about editing her book and I accepted. It was the type of self-help book I most admired, because it empowered its readers to shift their mentality out of victimhood and out of self-judgment — into self-acceptance.

I think of it as remembering who we truly are — and choosing to be that.

I picture myself, and all human beings, as beings of light, beings of energy. Down at the molecular level, of course that is true. We're all just electrons and protons and neutrons and other sub-atomic particles zipping through space, held together by electrical charges — and the God particle.

Somehow, some way, through a most intelligent design, a DNA code was created — and unique varieties of what we call human life sprung forth. And so we live our lives in the ways we were designed, and in the ways we were taught, and now we find ourselves here. We may have a job, a home, a family and friends — and each of those possibilities contain an infinite number of experiences. We discover that we live on a planet of extremes, one that allows for good and evil, love and hate, self-empowerment and self-loathing. And each one of us has the potential to embody all of the extremes at once — or not at all — or to take the middle path, the one of balance and the one that allows for the greatest good.

We drive our cars and drink our lattés and shoot people who scare us and make love to our partners and pull slivers out of our feet and taste guacamole and ride roller coasters and eat too much and stay awake watching television into the early hours of the next day.

And yet, we are still beings of light, beings of energy.

We stab worms onto hooks and take out the garbage and fly single-engine airplanes and drink a lot of beer and gaze at the sunset and mow the lawn and fart and walk the dog and protest in front of the Capitol and celebrate our birthdays and wake up and brush our teeth to start the day.

As beings of light, beings of energy, we do all of that — and much more.

Each of us is receiving and sending information at all times. And that information floods our being. Unfortunately, not much of this information seeps into our waking consciousness. Maybe an inkling that a parking spot right over there is open. Or a hunch that it's mom on the phone before it rings. I suggest that our bodies are flooded with light information at all times, and that only the slightest bit of detail is acted upon. Some of us are more attuned to these subtle energies than others.

Intuitives. Empaths. Mystics. Shamans. Healers. Meditators. Perhaps even physicists, like Albert Einstein, who said we use only a small percentage of our brains.

When we sleep, we connect with our true essence, and when we awaken, our true essence still exists. That innate intelligence connects globally — with others, with nature, with the world, with the universe — and locally — with our bodies, with our emotions and with our mind. Some refer to that innate intelligence as our higher self, but I like the description of it as an observing witness who is overseeing our personality and our decisions and our daily life, knowing full well that there are connections upon connections taking place within our person that are too complicated and probably too amazing for our personality selves to comprehend.

Spiritual leaders throughout time have taught us to reconnect with that inner witness — our true essence — through many tools and practices — and some of us do that intentionally, others do so intuitively, and most of us are not conscious at all that this is even possible.

How do I know that it is? Because sometimes I take a nap, wake up and then sit down in front of my computer and compose an article that I publish as a monthly column in The Edge, and minutes after writing such a piece, I could not for a second tell you where the idea or the information came from, other than to suggest that it was a part of my being that operates behind the scenes. I am convinced that if we are so attuned, a part of us can link with a powerfully creative flow of energy and produce that which we intend. It's no different than a songwriter who is inspired to write a string of songs in a short amount of time, or a painter who starts with a blank canvas and before long has layers of colors applied in a way that astounds even the creator.

Creative flow is free energy. It doesn't discern who uses it and for what reason. It just does what it does. If I tap into it, it may result in a written piece or an acrylic painting. If you tap into it, it may result in a dress design, or a song, or a sculpture, or a model for new currency based on the bartering of services. That free energy we tap into serves everyone equally. The only caveat is that we must participate. People who communicate with angels tell us that they can do miracles for us, but only if we ask. They do not intervene without our participation. The same goes for tapping into that unlimited creative flow. If we choose to engage with it, then it will flow through us and come out of us in our uniquely individual way.

We all have different words for this process, and for the source of the process. Some credit God or Jesus for all creation. I see it as a part of the software that comes with every human being who is born. Some are encouraged as children to tap into creativity, to believe in them and that incredible things are possible. Others are discouraged as children to use their imagination that life is about following the rules and never coloring outside of the lines. And even worse, some children are told that they are worthless and will never amount to anything.

To those children — many of whom are now fully functioning adults working as cashiers in convenience stores and investment bankers in skyscrapers and politicians in the government — I would love to scream from the rooftops to no longer accept the lies they have believed about themselves. I want to tell them that they are beautiful, loving beings. I want to tell them that by freeing themselves of limiting beliefs, their lives will transform miraculously into all that they choose to create.

This transformation may take lifetimes — or it may occur in the blink of an eye. I know, firsthand, that it is a challenge that requires courage and faith.

I was born in South Gate, California, just south of Los Angeles, in a hospital that no longer exists, to a risk-taking, twenty-something father who really didn't want me, and with a medical challenge that required major surgery at six months of age. Perhaps you've heard of Operation Smile or Smile Network International, which seek donations to provide surgical repair for children around the world who are born with cleft lips and palates. I was one such child. With the ever-loving support of my mom, and children's hospitals that help children in need, I went through a dozen major surgeries by the time I was 14 and was given a repaired soft palate using cartilage from a rib, a revised upper lip and nose, as well as dental care that helped to replace two teeth missing since birth.

Very few people know that I have had such experiences. But inwardly, the personal judgment and schoolhouse ridicule left a lingering residue that I still re-experience sometimes when I'm feeling blue. In public, if someone stares at me too long, my mind tells me they are judging how I look. In reality, maybe they are attracted to the light in my aura. Things are rarely what we think they are.

Yes, at times I accepted the victim mentality. But I have long since learned to empower myself by tapping into my creativity and finding joy in creating something new. I continue to find new things to learn and challenge myself to keep striving onward, and upward. My growing edge is to fully embody the victor within and stand tall in support of who I truly am. I'm not quite there yet.

During my first year of college, one day I was leaving a building and ran into my speech teacher. Observing me, most likely walking with my head held low, he said, "Stand tall, Tim. You are a tall man."

One night I had a lucid dream in which it was dark and I was walking downtown somewhere. On the corner, I heard music and laughter and walked into a nightspot that featured poetry, beatniks and a free exchange of dialogue. People were creative and spontaneous, and they felt loose and free and supported in what they had to express. I found myself walking down a sidewalk and up to the front door of a house, where my girlfriend lived, though in real life she did not exist. I opened the door and walked down the stairs to the basement. I stood in the center of the basement, and suddenly a blast of energy moved my body across the floor to the other side of the room, and I heard the words, "You have the power," and then I woke up suddenly and sat up in bed.

I've never forgotten that experience, because inwardly, I knew it was true. I knew the observing witness was trying to get my attention, trying to kick start my conscious awareness of how empowered I truly am. Sometimes dreams can have that effect. Sometimes other people can have that effect. And sometimes you just don't know how the inspiration will manifest.

The key is to be awake. It's easy to keep hitting the snooze button of life, but it's much more fun and more enlivening to participate. Thanks to all of the wonderful co-creators in this book, it's now a little bit easier to become inspired, to keep carrying water and chopping wood, to keep marching to the beat of my own drummer and staying in my heart as often as I can.

Tim Miejan is a 28-year veteran of print media. He is editor and co-publisher of *The Edge* magazine, a monthly publication dedicated to holistic living that has served the Upper Midwest USA since 1992. He also manages online resources for *The Edge* magazine and *Edge Life Expos & Events*, and he is a freelance editor, writer and graphic designer.

He graduated from high school in Norfolk, NE, and is a graduate of Missouri Western State University, in St. Joseph, MO. He served for 12 years as a reporter and editor for the *St. Joseph News-Press*, St. Joseph, Missouri, a daily newspaper serving Northwest Missouri. In 1995, he moved to the Twin Cities of Minneapolis and St. Paul, Minnesota, and became managing editor of *The Edge*, a free monthly periodical promoting personal growth, integrative healing, and global transformation.

His interviews of notable leaders in consciousness and healing have been reprinted by online publications in Germany and Italy, and in print magazines *Advaita Journal* (Germany) and *Stoppinder: A Gurdjieff Journal for Our Time*. He was the editor and co-author of the book, *A Victim No More*, with Lori Rekowski. His writing is included in *Angel Cats: Divine Messengers of Comfort* (New World Library, 2004).

Tim currently lives in Madison, WI, and shares his life with his loving wife Rachel, stepson Kyle, and his cats, Sunti and Cleo. He has traveled to Great Britain, Venezuala and throughout the United States, and enjoys filmmaking, photography, walking and reading.

www.miejan.com
www.facebook.com/miejan

Meet Karen Mayfield of *Wake Up Women*

Wake up Women
Be Happy Healthy Wealthy
Have Peace of Mind
And live a life you love . . .

FOR MANY YEARS I have had this knowing, a calling some would call it. I get glimpses into the future of things that eventually transpire. I later discovered I was actually remote viewing. I found it very interesting that I was doing something that I had no knowledge even existed. These glimpses or snapshots of the future made no sense when they occurred, but I just learned to go with it and not question why, just move forward and trust that there was a meaning to this supposed madness.

It all started when I was forty-seven and started seeing the number 11, this was as strange as the remote viewing, however it was happening so frequently that I knew something bigger than what could meet the eye was happening. After a life-threatening illness, I started praying every time I would see the number eleven. I actually changed the entire way I prayed — instead of praying the begging prayer, I changed it to the gratitude prayer — and soon positive changes started happening in my life.

For several years, I had taught a personal growth course called Peace of Mind but had never actually taken the course myself. People who had taken the course experienced miraculous transformations in their lives, so I to became a student of my own work. This course actually puts the Laws of Attraction in fast forward motion, and I was about to see manifestation in its highest form, when things I only dreamed of actually became a reality. This course is now taught as the Wake up Women coaching course and is the center of our coaching division called the Giving Foundation.

Now, ten years later, the life I live is very different then the life I had lived previously. I am not going to tell you that it is all roses but I know everything happens for a reason. To quote Napoleon Hill, "Within every adversity there is an equal to or greater benefit. We just have to have the belief and the foresight to know it."

In 2007, I saw the words, "Wake up Women" for the first time used together and I inherently knew that it was no accident. Within a year, the first Wake up Women book was being released and before long it was a best seller, and the rest, as they say, is history. At that time, Social Media was beginning to dominate and grow exponentially and platforms like MySpace, LinkedIn, Yahoo groups, Google, and soon Facebook would become day-to-day methods of sharing our personal lives with the world. Share and share alike has new meaning, and connecting with family and making new friends has turned into a global playground.

In 2011 after much encouragement, I decided it was time to start the Wake up Women fan page. I really wasn't into social media or Facebook that much, and on my personal page I had less than 300 friends. But fan pages were all the rage and I was ready to catch the wave and see what would happen. After doing a Facebook search, I found that there was already a Wake up Women fan page that also had about 300 fans. Instead of being upset that this page existed, I read every post, I loved everything I read. I could not have done it better so why try?

It was then I looked for the page owner and found Saba Agha, who lives half away across the planet from me. Her life could not have been more different then mine, but we had this common thread that bound us, Wake up Women. However, I did not immediately contact Saba. I prayed several days for discernment. You see, Saba is a Muslim, I had been raised a Christian, and even though I was a metaphysician, all of a sudden, I was fearful of moving forward. But I knew this was no accident and I needed to trust the Universe. After days of deliberation the only message I received from the universe was if you turn them off, you will turn them away. I knew I had to contact Saba and introduce myself and see what would happen. Let me say Saba is the most loving person I have never met in person, but we were joined together on purpose and that purpose was Wake up Women. Literally, this was a match made in heaven. Saba is now our Chief Transformational Officer and is a very intricate part of the Wake up Women team.

Before long, we were celebrating 10,000 fans, then 20,000 we even wrote two Wake up Women books crowd-sourcing our fans, called Flashbooks. We were rocking this page and connecting with women all over the world. Our message was making a impact, and then it happened. On February 24, 2012 we woke up and someone had hacked our Facebook page. It was the closest thing to a hostile take-over I have ever experienced. We contacted Facebook, got on the forums and Saba and I prayed more than 5 times a day facing Mecca, we prayed incessantly for divine guidance. Finally, after some time we were resigned to start back with a new page. Saba and our other admin Judy, as well as Saba's husband Hassan launched our fan page once again. I stayed behind on Facebook and worked every day to attempt to get our page back from the hacker but finally after a very exhausting effort I gave it up and joined the rest of the team on our new page.

I realized we were doing something right or they would have never attempted to shut us down or try to stop us. But our mission was bigger than any hacker was. Starting back over at Zero was very difficult for each of us, but we persevered and at the time of writing this story, we are nearing 10,000 fans in less than 3 months.

The hacking did not stop there. Within two months after our Facebook page, the same people hacked the Wake up Women web site. Unfortunately for the hacker, this time they did not get away with it. Within minutes of them hacking the site I happened to log on and found it looked totally different then it had just 15 minutes earlier. I also noticed the same picture placed on the front page was the same on the Facebook page. It was Sunday, so for 18 hours I was left with the sinking feeling that once again someone was trying to stop us from doing what we knew we were supposed to do. On Monday morning, I contacted our web hosting company, we were able to isolate the ISP address they had used, and within minutes, our web site was returned to us, unlike our original Facebook page.

The next miracle that would come our way was on the morning of June 7 2012. I received a Google alert. Wake up Women is trademarked, so each time the words, "Wake up Women" are placed together in a sentence I get a Google alert. Even more interesting I received this alert one-year to the date of finding Saba and the Wake up Women fan page. Most of the time these alerts are of little significance but not this one.

This alert read Wake up Women victory conference and there was a web site, so I clicked on it and discovered Ms. BeBee Watson. Playing in the background is a Wake up Women song that BeBee wrote, composed, and performed. Once again I loved everything about it. Just 5 days before receiving this Google alert, I had decided it was time to take the Wake up Women message on tour, and just like placing a order to the universe, I found BeBee. Before long, she and I engaged in a 4-hour conversation and just like Saba, our message was the same. I knew I had found another collaborator for Wake up Women. Soon, we will be hosting Wake up Women Victory Conferences all over the word and the message of hope, domestic peace and equality will span the globe.

The Wake up Women core team consists of a Woman from the Middle East that is Muslim, part African American Woman from the United States that is a Christian Evangelist and a white metaphysician woman (myself) sharing a message for Women that will change the lives of Women forever. I am sure a Jewish woman will be joining us and the tapestry of Wake up Women will be woven together with the thread of sisterhood and family like no other.

2012 has proven to be a year of trials, & tribulations placed upon us by forces that do not want us doing what we are doing. But in spite of it all, the Wake up Women journey has been one of miracle-type events. Unlike any other membership in the world we have launched our coaching division that helps our members discover their passion and purpose. With the interactive blueprint and active ingredient to the Laws of attraction, and with our unique software, we are able to assist our member in funding their dreams, relieving their debt, and empowering their lives by just designating 60% of our gross income to be distributed back to our members. The Wake up Women radio show is hosted each Saturday and offers women and men the opportunity to hear from leading authorities as they share their golden nuggets of wisdom with our audience.

Now, more determined than ever, we are on our mission sharing inspiring, instructing, and informing women that they can Be happy, Be healthy, Be wealthy have Peace of Mind and Live a life they love free from oppression or religious differences. By connecting like a vine and spreading like a virus our message, women are beginning to Wake up all over the world to their power. Join us in the wonderful world of Wake up Women and experience the life that is waiting for you ...

Until Next time . . .

Karen Mayfield Msc.CC

Karen Mayfield is a CTA certified coach, Metaphysical Minister, creator of the Peace of Mind Principles online Coaching program and personal growth seminars, co-author in the *Wake up: Live the Life You Love* best selling book series, and co-creator and publisher in the Wake up Women book series and co-owner in Wake up Women BE. Karen is a former Mars Venus facilitator and relationship coach. Her twenty years of experience in print advertising, ad copy, and print media campaigns, combined with her fifteen years in training and mid to upper management provides Karen with the background in niche marketing needed in today's spiritually emerging market and economy. Karen is co-creator of Wake up Coaches, Wake up Women, OVEMENT that ultimately allows people the experience of Peace of Mind as a state of mind. She is also the creator of *You've Got Prayer,* a global prayer link for peace, harmony, hope, and gratitude. Being a mom, grandmother, friend, and member in a family of Entrepreneurial women is the inspiration behind Karen's purpose. "When you help women you help the world." Karen loves assisting others in building a foundation of spiritual healing and enlightenment, financial freedom, physical health, emotional wellness, family harmony, and career purpose following the Peace of Mind Principles.

http://wakeupwomen.com
http://www.thegivingfoundation.com

Meet Bebee Watson

Motivational Speaker, Author, Psalmist Bebee Watson Inspires The Masses While Embracing Her Journey

BEBEE WATSON KNEW THAT she had a calling on her life at a very young age. She can remember when she started hearing the Voice of God and seeing visions. Her grandmother told her that she was a very special child and God's Hand was on her life and He would show her His Will. With that, she would simply send her to bed and assured her that sooner or later, "you will know."

By the time she was in her early 20's she began to see the visions and dreams coming to pass in her life. After completing school and starting her own family she took the back seat to see where her life would go. She had a lot of faith in what she believed and what God was calling her to do, but her spirit was still not satisfied. Bebee Watson knows what it's like to be a broken and hurting woman as she ministers from personal life experiences. From a broken home and her house burning down to the ground, from losing everything including her mother to cancer and family walking away, while sickness tried to consumer her body... she *clearly* has a story to tell. It was during this time she witnessed His Healing Power with her eight-month-old son whom died in her arms. On their drive to the hospital, being twenty minutes away, the tire blew out on the car. She immediately heard the spirit speak and ask her, "DO YOU BELIEVE IN MY MIRACLES?" Her spirit knew she had no other choice but to trust what he was asking her and come face to face with her faith. She then got out of the car, laid her baby across the hood, stretched forth her hands and began to pray for him. In just a short matter of time he coughed and God restored her son back to life! Not knowing this was *only the beginning* of many more miracles to come!

At that point she knew there was no turning back, no matter what the cost. She heeded to the Voice of God and accepted the Call on her life, unaware of the price she would have to pay. Not only was her son's life threatened, but her body was attacked as well. With various doctors unable to diagnose her symptoms for many months, in the year 2000, she was diagnosed with cancer. However, after eighteen months of battling, she continued to hold on to what she believed in, clinging to God's Promises and not accepting that prognosis for her life. She turned her plate down and began praying and confessing her healing. Then late one night in 2001 around 3A.M. she felt a burning sensation, like "fire" she recalls, shoot straight through her body. She knew that she had been healed. She remains cancer free to this day. This is merely a glimpse of the cost she has paid for the Anointing on her life. She has "gave it all up," and has witnessed first-hand that it profits a man nothing to gain the world and lose his soul. She is a walking testimony of "laying it all down" and continues to impact and help bring a "life change" to many. He has gifted her to lay hands on the sick and see them restored, even through the power of "blowing" the Anointing of God upon them. She has witnessed cancer patients healed, lymphatic fluid dry up, the bi-polar and mental-stricken set free, Crohn's disease demolished, the lame able to walk, the deaf healed, the dead raised, health regained from strokes, deliverance from HIV, alcohol additions, demons cast out and much, much more. It has been spoken over her time and time again that she is truly *God's leaping angel*...

Dating back to the early 90's the Lord has given her prophecy on top of prophecy from around the world and has shown her visions to unlock them. She has captured in numerous, priceless journals, conversations with God, where He has confirmed His Plans and Promises for her life. During this time He birthed BBW Ministries, a deliverance ministry created to impact the world, empower your spirit and embrace your soul!

Watson's talk show, "Can A Sister Talk To You?" (based on her book of the same name) is now airing worldwide. With a desire to see God's women rise up and live the lives they were called to live.

Bebee states, "'Can A Sister Talk To You' was given to me to help not only women, but men as well. Ministering to the lost, the hurt or those with unanswered questions, I want to help them understand that they don't have to stay where they are. It's not about where you are, but where God wants to take you."

With the assistance of her teachings, her listener's witness healing, breakthroughs, and wisdom, to help carry them while on their journey. With topics such as "DNA: Drama Needs Attention, Just ask Jezebel" or "Scars In The Mirror" her faithful listening audience is over 500,000 and most recently made the Top 50 Best Black Blogs for African Americans in 2012.

She is also the Founder/CEO of *Embrace Magazine, Assedo Records,* "*balo*" greeting card line, as well as the charitable organization, "*Faith of an Angel.*" Faith of an Angel specializes in hosting Benefits Concerts for children with disabilities, sickness and diseases throughout the country. In 2012, she launched the women's conference, *Wake Up, Women! Victory Conference* taken from her book, *Can A Sister Talk To You?* She has also released her EP "*Eventualities*" featuring the hit song of the conference, *Wake Up Women.* She has traveled the globe doing many seminars and conference to equip women for a better tomorrow. Watson is a key-note speaker for the *A Victim No More* conference scheduled to kick off Fall, 2012 in Orlando, Florida then traveling worldwide.

She has appeared on the following television stations as well: TBN, Dove Broadcasting, Babbie's House with Babbie Mason, WATC-Atlanta Live, WBPI-Club 36 with Dorothy Spaulding and TCT's Rejoice as well as featured in articles in local and national newspapers, magazines and radio stations.

Watson holds degrees in Education, Counseling, Management and a Ministerial degree from Rhema University. She is licensed and ordained by the Redemption Ministerial Fellowship (Redemption World Outreach) under the leadership of Apostle Ron Carpenter, Jr. and Bishop Paul Gaehring as well as Bishop David M. Callands, Jr. of the Issachar Covenant Fellowship of Churches.

Each day is a new opportunity for her to use her God-given gifts combined with her unique style to reach audiences of all backgrounds, as she is most comfortable amongst the *real* people.

 Bebee Watson is a Motivational Speaker, Author, Psalmist called to inspire the masses while embracing her journey. To help women understand that they don't have to stay where they are. It's not about where you are, but where God wants to take you. Seeing a complacency and spiritual lethargy in some of today's women, Bebee Watson has a desire to see women rise up and live the lives they were called to live. She has traveled the globe doing many seminars and conference to equip women for a better tomorrow. She has appeared on the following television stations as well: TBN, Dove Broadcasting, *Babbie's House with Babbie Mason*, WATC-Atlanta Live, WBPI-Club 36 with Dorothy Spaulding and TCT's *Rejoice* as well as featured in articles in local and national newspapers, magazines and radio stations.

https://www.facebook.com/bebee.watson
https://www.facebook.com/bebeewatson2
http://www.bbwministries.org
http://www.canasistertalktoyou.com
http://www.bebeewatson.info
http://www.wakeupwomenconference.com

Meet Alexa Heilbron Oritz of
Your Beautiful Life

"Who is Alexa Heilbron Ortiz?" progressively has become an easier question for me to answer. My journey of self-discovery and personal growth during the past few years has allowed me to reach a point where I now understand who I am, who I once was, and the person I am yet to become. Now, I can happily tell you not only who I am, but the reasons behind the very essence of "me." However, this wasn't always the case. I must admit that for some time — and maybe for longer than I would have once liked to acknowledge — I had no idea who I was.

My road to self-acceptance was paved by circumstances that occurred during my teenage years and into my early adulthood. These life events were not ones that I would classify as tragic or catastrophic, but they were significant enough to change who I would become — forever. I didn't know it then, but those years would eventually be the catalyst that would inspire me to grow, learn and accept all that life would bring my way. It was because of these events that I would make the conscious decision to not allow any circumstances to define me or the life

I desired to live. I was fortunate enough to discover the power of inner strength, while simultaneously being blessed with the love and compassion of those whom I met along the way.

My childhood was a beautiful one, filled with fond memories and special moments. I grew up in a two-parent household in which I was unconditionally loved, protected and cared for in the best way that my parents knew how. I was raised with the idealistic notion that I could be anything or anyone I wanted to be, so long as I worked diligently towards my dreams, stayed true to myself, and treated others with respect and compassion. Having a strong foundation beneath me, and the guiding principles of my loving family ingrained within me, I lived in a world that I perceived as fair, happy and safe. That was until my family suffered a great financial loss. My parents had owned a successful business for most of their lives, and they had always been able to provide for our family. In a series of events that I was too young to understand, my parents' dream life and hard work crumbled before their eyes. The details of their company's demise are not ones that will make a difference in my story, but their aftermath of loss and emotional struggles would inevitably shape my life.

Shortly after all this occurred, my parents explained to my siblings and me that things would be changing in our home, from a financial perspective. Their words were one big blur that I couldn't understand or comprehend, much less process, but in the mist of my confusion, I knew that I would never be the same. My seemingly normal reality was about to be altered — and little did I know that during this process, I would lose the first man I ever loved, the one person who had never let me down, the man I called my father. Nothing or no one could have prepared me for the fact that I would lose my dad to depression, self-loathing and mental unrest.

To make this very long story short, I will go on to tell you that this pivotal moment in our lives broke my father to the very core of his existence, and he was never the same again. From that point on, and for reasons I could not understand, my father began to displace his anger, resentment and grief on me. Life at home was unbearable. My new reality was one I could not fathom, and the harder I tried to make things better with my dad, the worse they ultimately became. My mom was too busy working and trying to figure out how we were going to survive to realize what I was experiencing. My siblings, who are much older, had moved out by this point and were not aware of the life I was living at home. My relationship with my dad became non-existent. He had become withdrawn, unmotivated and cold, and he was no longer someone I recognized. At the time, I didn't understand what he was going through. Instead, I internalized his actions and blamed myself for his behavior.

When I went away to college, I was angry, and I resented my family for "destroying" my life. I still could not understand why things had so drastically changed and what had happened to my father. I can say with certainty that during this time my transformation began. During my years in college, I purposely isolated myself from my immediate family and dove into my studies. I developed a love for psychology, and the study of human behavior; it became my passion, my guiding force and my ultimate salvation.

Out of a place of anger and resentment grew an intense curiosity and interest in the human mind, and before I knew it, feelings of sadness, rejection and self-pity began to transform into compassion, love and — most importantly — forgiveness. During my time away from home, I was blessed with amazing friends, great mentors and people who genuinely cared for me. Their care and compassion for me was so powerful and pure that everything in me yearned to change. I cannot tell you how or when I was able to break free of all that was tying me down, but before long I began to feel my true self emerge, as I learned to forgive, as I allowed myself to heal from the inside out.

Upon my return from college, things at home had become more chaotic. My father's health rapidly declined, and eventually he was placed in a nursing facility, suffering from severe depression and the early onset of Alzheimer's. Ironically, it was during those years of instability and uncertainty when I discovered myself — and my purpose. I vowed to not permit the circumstances surrounding my life to determine the person I would become. I felt a need to be there for others. I wanted to become a guiding light, a compassionate friend, to anyone who was in need of love and support. Forgiveness and acceptance became my driving force and guiding principles. And I also realized that I would need to connect deeply into the core of who I truly am if ever I was to forgive my father, understand my mother and accept my reality for what it was. I was willing to look past their imperfections — and choices — and I began to believe in the resiliency of the human spirit.

Fast forward 10 years and I can honestly say that life has been so good to me. I am blessed in so many ways that it would require the writing of an entirely separate book to begin to describe the beautiful experiences with which life has showered me. That being said, I can reveal this: Helping out others and inspiring those around me to live happy and peaceful lives has been my rhyme and reason since entering the professional world. I am a social worker and have been so for seven years. I spend my days working with people who have suffered terrible tragedies and have lived with drug addictions for many years. I dearly love this rewarding and life-altering career.

Four months ago, I began to experience a desire to do more. I longed to help others and I wanted to spread the message of love and hope to as many people as I could reach. This inspired thought led me to create a motivational page on Facebook — and from this, Your Beautiful Life [www.facebook.com/Yourbeautifullife] was born. Like a child, within days it began to have a life of its own. The response was breathtaking. I was amazed and completely awestruck by the gratitude of those with whom I came in contact. Clearly, people were in need of a reassuring word or a positive thought — something to believe in.

It wasn't long before I understood that I had found my calling: Bringing hope, love and peace to those who need it was what I had been called to do. I am humbled by the fact that so many people have allowed me to walk beside them on their very personal journeys, and it is an honor to be allowed into their lives. My passion to inspire — and my ability to touch so many lives — keeps my soul alive and thriving. My hope is to continue to inspire thousands, maybe even millions, of people to live, love, and enjoy their beautiful lives.

Alexa Heilbron is a proud mother of two happy and energetic young boys. She is employed as a full-time Social Worker for Dependency Drug Court in Miami, Florida. For the past 7 years she has been working closely with families who are involved in the social welfare system due to substance abuse, mental health issues and domestic violence problems. Although her job is at times challenging, she describes her work as humbling and extremely rewarding. Approximately 5 months ago Alexa started the motivational page *Your Beautiful Life* with the hopes of providing inspiration and inner peace to those who needed it the most. Her passion to inspire is one driven by her love and gratitude towards life and her belief in the resiliency of the human spirit. It is her wish for all her subscribers to live, love and enjoy their beautiful lives.

www.facebook.com/YourBeautifulLife

Meet Scott Hacker of *Taboo Jive*

I CREATED TABOOJIVE as a way to spark spirited, vibrant conversations about overlooked or repressed aspects of contemporary culture. My intention is to encourage anyone to freely participate, to "say your piece" within stimulating discussions of taboo and controversial topics, for the sake of education, awareness, enlightenment, and entertainment.

Although the idea for Taboojive was inspired by recent conversations, the desire to foster these liberating discussions stems back to the days when I was a child growing up on a farm in a rural small town of the mid-western United States. Several factors stand out from that time, including being bullied, marginalized, and experiencing physical discipline, as well as being aware of racist, sexist, and homophobic attitudes. Perhaps what most motivated me to eventually question taboo topics, though, was my upbringing within fundamentalist Christianity.

My grandfather was the pastor of the tiny Baptist church I attended. Every Sunday, my grandpa passionately preached about 'being saved,' how we need to find God in order to get into Heaven because Satan and Hell were just waiting for us given our sinful ways. I remember feeling a strange mix of fear, guilt, and a fuzzy sense of shame about never quite being good enough. To be clear, I love my grandpa. Looking back I see that he wanted to do the right thing, and he taught these things because he really believed them. However, I have also come to see that he didn't realize the damage that often results.

The guilt feelings instilled by many of these fundamentalist religions keep people trapped in feelings of unworthiness and self-doubt. I have come to see this as a form of indoctrination that encourages you to blindly conform, to follow other people or teachings – especially if they're not healthy for you -- because you don't fully trust and love yourself.

As a child, raised within a fundamentalist church, I didn't have a choice about what I was allowed to believe. From a young age, though, many of these teachings did not resonate with me. I also remember being disheartened by often intolerant or judgmental comments made by too many church members, even as they smiled about how Jesus loves us. My own experiences, such as a period of time when I was bullied, provided a frame of reference to appreciate the pain of harmful attitudes that divide and disrespect groups of people. Gradually, I began to see the ways these beliefs limited me and the more I learned, the more questions I asked and answers I sought, not only to theological questions but other controversial, "taboo" topics.

It took me quite some time to detoxify from the programming of my religious upbringing. The first step away from this limiting mindset was a move from my small hometown, which offered an opportunity to become aware of more opinions and perspectives. After pursuing an engineering CNC machinist career for a number of years, I quit my job and moved to Florida to pursue my dream of a professional golf career. This choice was very freeing and enhanced the quality of my life in ways I never imagined possible. I eventually went on to achieve this dream, as least partly; to date I have had the pleasurable experience of winning six minor-league tournaments as well as achieving many top 5 and 10 finishes. Not too bad considering my last name is "Hacker!"

In the fall of 2008, I met my life partner Betty Woodman, a grad student and instructor of philosophical topics, who went on to attain her Ph.D. at Emory University in the spring of 2012. Among other topics, Betty had studied religions and their histories. She was able to educate me about aspects of the history of Christianity that had been overlooked in my religious upbringing. In addition, Betty distinguishes the strengthening potential of spiritual practices from dynamics that foster blind conformity. Our conversations helped me separate the empowering aspects of religious thought from fundamentalist religious dogma and thus enabled me to embrace a spiritual path.

Occasionally Betty, her son Ryan, and I would sit around and engage in thought- provoking discussions about various controversial topics. I have to admit, especially at first, I didn't always agree with the myriad of views and opinions that were brought up within the discussions, but it was intriguing to hear and entertain new perspectives, philosophies, and approaches. We discussed everything from politics and religion to sexuality and organic foods, from UFOs and aliens to witches, the paranormal, and paganism, from the history and customs of societies and the ways they promote or constrain freedom to emerging trends in contemporary culture. We were all over the map, and it felt good to be in this space of openness, honesty, and respect for differing opinions. This was new! And it felt really great.

The idea for Taboojive came to me one evening during one of our chats. I wondered if there were more people out there who might feel the same way about these discussions. I started to ponder ways I might position some of these lesser-known topics for discussion with others who may be interested in learning and exploring. Although these topics are ones that many families can't or don't typically talk about around the dinner table, people are hungry to talk about them.

At first I posted a few of these topics to my personal Facebook page. However, instead of sparking organic discussion, I received negative feedback from some friends and family with the old mindset, who thought I was crazy for wanting to openly discuss and question these taboo topics. Realizing this wouldn't be the best way to approach the discussion, I began to think about a creative, catchy, interesting name for an Internet forum. Within a few days, I had "Taboo Jive!" The word 'taboo' has a guilty pleasure connotation and lures a curious person in to see what our website and forum are all about. The word 'Jive' of course is just a cool or slang expression for 'talk' or vibe.

In 2011, I launched taboojive.com as a website. It didn't take more than a few months for us to gain a real following of fun, engaged fans, who were interacting on both the website and Facebook fan page. The internet, and Facebook in particular, present incredible opportunities for learning, support, and networking. Our fan base grew through networking through other fan pages with shared philosophies. These include particularly the Wipe Out Homophobia fan page. Since Taboojive supports the LGBT community, as well as equal rights and social justice in general, we wrote and published a favorable review of their website and forum. From this we gained a large number of fans who appreciate a forum where people discuss controversial topics through civil and respectful discourse.

Wonderfully, Taboo Jive has come together the way I imagined it. We currently have individuals from over forty countries following us. Our posts and discussion topics encourage organic, tumbling conversations reflecting a rich diversity of ideas, philosophies, opinions, and perspectives contributed by participants from many different places. Not only are we lucky enough to have a large interactive fan base, but our statistics reveal that we have many people who follow our discussions anonymously, perhaps to learn from the different perspectives and conversations.

Taboojive has benefited from people who have helped it along from the beginning, particularly Drew Cumens, our website techy guy, Robert Mynatt, writer and contributing admin, and all our wonderful contributing writers. Betty's son, Ryan Kohlsdorf, and his open-minded discussions of varied topics inspired the idea for Taboo Jive. My partner, Betty continues to contribute so much through her insight, sensitivity to all forms of unhealthy power dynamics, and commitment to empowerment.

I look forward to continuing to grow our forum in a positive direction. Taboojive encourages discussion and debate, and participants overwhelmingly adhere to our request for respectful, civil discourse as ground rules for the conversations. Differing opinions and views allow for more learning all around. There are so many topics of conversation that remain suppressed and forbidden to talk about. However, we need to talk about these issues and topics in order to keep learning, growing, and moving forward in ways that benefit everyone. I encourage everyone to expand their views by considering additional perspectives on issues, even if this means looking outside their churches, schools, and normal media sources. Education and learning represent no threat; more knowledge and awareness simply offers a broader perspective so that you may make your own best informed decisions about what you think, feel, or believe. Some may find, as I did, that new perspectives broaden your appreciation of the bigger picture. It also may reveal ways you have been limiting yourselves or allowing others to constrain your abilities and expression.

Throughout this journey, I've really come to appreciate the value of an open mind and a broader view, and so I continually seek new information, additional perspectives, and more connections with fellow travelers. Come join the discussion at our taboojive.com Facebook fan page. Whatever your view, we invite you to "say your piece."

 Scott Hacker is a minor-league golf professional and the creator, founder, and curator of *Taboojive.com*, a website that promotes consideration of controversial and lesser known topics. A native of southwest Michigan now living in Atlanta, GA, Scott is an athlete who aspires to play and compete at the highest levels of the golfing world. At the same time he is an avid learner and seeker of knowledge. Scott's website and fan page provide resources for those who, like himself, desire to become more aware of topics that are often suppressed or deemed forbidden, controversial, or taboo by contemporary culture.

taboojive.com
www.facebook.com/TabooJive

Meet Lissa Coffey of *Coffey Talk*

CLOSURE: Coming Full Circle

EACH OF US EXPERIENCES some kind of loss in this lifetime. People come and go from our lives, whether by choice or circumstance. How we cope with these events affects how we move forward, how we see the world, and how we feel about our lives.

I'm not the only person to have been through a divorce. When my first marriage ended after 17 years, I thought I handled it well. It was an amicable parting, and we maintained a friendly relationship. But then a few years later my sister's husband died unexpectedly. My grief brought up new emotions, and I felt sad and angry and hurt as I relived the divorce in my mind. I realized through this experience that although I had moved on, I hadn't really gotten over it; I didn't have closure. I saw the parallels between my sister's loss and my own, and I actively sought to come up with a formula through which we could both alleviate our pain.

Relationships take many forms: marriage, friendships, family, co-workers, classmates, lovers. Whenever two people have some kind of a connection, a relationship is established. Our energy goes into these connections, our emotions, our hopes, our human vulnerabilities. A relationship is an organism itself, and it can have a life cycle. But since relationship is a spiritual organism, it doesn't die. It merely changes shape. The relationships we build with the people we encounter continue in spirit, in memories, and in lessons learned.

We are invested in our relationships with other people. We spend our time, and emotions, developing a kind of bond with a person. We give of ourselves, through our love, our friendship, our concern, and our efforts.

When we are faced with what seems to be the "end" of a relationship, we may feel loss, grief, anger or pain. We might even feel relief, or freedom. We may question the purpose for this change, whether it is abrupt or expected, and the necessity of it. The change may or may not be our choice, or our desire, but something we must learn to live with. The uneasiness may nag at us for years as we struggle to understand. How do we get that "closure" that our hearts and minds so desperately seek so that we can move forward with our lives?

We need to shift our perspective a little bit when it comes to relationships. In our human form, we see the illusion of death, and the ending of relationships. But what really takes place is a transformation. As we learn and grow through our relationships, our relationships evolve. We can use this evolution as an opportunity for continued growth, and for personal transformation. The pains that we feel are growing pains. However a relationship changes, whether it is a loss from physical death, a divorce, a move away, a growing up, or a falling out, we can not only survive, but thrive, knowing that everything, always, is exactly the way it is meant to be.

A Natural Law works whether we are aware of it or not. It is a principle of nature that is in effect at all times, without favoritism. Gravity is a natural law. It works the same for everyone, at all times. By being aware of gravity, we can move about more freely, with less risk of pain from falling down.

The Law of Relationship is two-fold. It says:

1) We are all connected.
2) We are here to help each other.

We are all connected in one-way or another. We feel the same emotions; we share the same experiences. We are brothers and sisters on this planet. This connection bonds us, and gives us a relationship with each other. A mother in any part the world, can relate to another mother she has never seen because she knows what it means, and how it feels, to be a mother. We are all born the same way, and have to learn how to walk and talk and find our way in the world. We face challenges and heartache, no matter where we live, or how we live. Our connection cannot be broken.

With our challenges and experiences we learn and grow. Our relationships bring us many challenges and experiences, and through our relationships we learn and grow. This is how we help each other. We may not even know that we are doing it, but just by being in a person's life, in some small way, we are contributing to the learning process, as they are contributing to ours. Our actions affect other people in ways we can't even imagine. Even in times when we feel hurt by someone, that is an opportunity for us to learn and grow. We might not realize it in the moment, but in some strange and miraculous way, we are helping each other by going through this experience together.

Closure is different than grief. Grieving is looking back; closure is about looking ahead. We want to let go and move on. This is what closure gives us. We may have gone through the grieving process and still not have the closure we seek. The law of relationship helps us to maneuver our way through the five set process of closure: Recognition, Acceptance, Understanding, Integration, and Gratitude. When we reach a feeling of gratitude, we know we've come full circle to experience closure.

Closure is actually the perfect word for it. It's more than neatly tying up loose ends. Think about life as a series of events and relationships, all linked together in some sort of artistic way, like a beautiful piece of jewelry. We can't wear a necklace or a bracelet if the chain is just left dangling. The jewelry maker finishes off the piece by adding a clasp, one loop that kind of ties together the beginning and the end, the start and the finish, so that what we are left with is one strong continuous chain. Our closure is that clasp. Closure helps it all make sense. It turns something seemingly broken into something useful, purposeful, and lovely.

Be the Dog

Years ago, my sister Marci started a new job—her dream job at the time. She called me giddy with excitement; she could hardly wait to start. But her enthusiasm soon deflated when she was met with a lot of resistance at her office. I called to check on her after a few days to see how the new position was going. She was miserable. Marci said that although she loved the work, and knew she could really contribute, she felt like the other people in the office didn't like her. They had already formed their little cliques and she felt like an outsider. She was very uncomfortable with this situation and was having a hard time functioning in that kind of an environment.

The advice I gave her was this: "Be the Dog." Basically, the way I saw the situation, the people in her office were acting like cats. When Marci came into the room, they would toss their tails in the air and walk in the other direction, arch their backs, or even hiss. Rather than to try to be a cat and fit in with this group, Marci needed to take a vastly different approach. She needed to be the dog. She needed to bounce into the room with her tail wagging, full of energy and with a big smile on her face. That's how a dog is. A dog isn't aloof. He doesn't wait for you to be his friend; he assumes you already are his friend! He approaches with enthusiasm. I told Marci to take on this attitude and see what happened.

Sure enough, in a few days the whole energy around the office shifted. How could anyone not accept a happy and loving dog? She had all those cats purring! Once she had built up positive relationships with her co-workers, she was able to work more efficiently and effectively. It was a better working environment for everyone.

Lissa Coffey is a Lifestyle and Relationship Expert who serves up an inspiring blend of ancient wisdom and modern style on her website *CoffeyTalk.com* and in her e-mail newsletters. She is the host of a web series that is on youtube, blinkx and other online outlets. Lissa is a bestselling author, her most recent book is: *What's Your Dharma? Discover the Vedic Way to Your Life's Purpose.* Lissa is often called the "Dosha Diva"—she is world renown as the authority on Ayurveda and Relationships. Her book on the topic is *What's Your Dosha, Baby? Discover the Vedic Way for Compatibility in Life and Love.* A sought-after guest expert, Lissa Coffey appears frequently on television and radio and contributes to many national publications with her insightful and compassionate approach to modern-day issues. Her e-mail newsletters are enjoyed around the world by a steadily growing subscriber base.

https://www.facebook.com/lissa.coffey?ref=ts
https://www.facebook.com/LissaCoffeyTalk
http://www.CoffeyTalk.com
http://www.ClosureBook.com
http://www.WhatsYourDosha.com
http://www.PSMeditation.com
http://www.FamilyEveryday.com
http://www.DoshaDesign.com

Meet Debra Puglisi Sharp

My MISSION IN LIFE is to empower victims to become survivors. I did not ask to become a victim. However, I chose to reclaim my life after trauma and am pleased to have this opportunity to share my story of courage, hope, and faith with all of you.

Without dwelling on my victimization, I will briefly summarize the details of an event that changed my life forever. I am not the same person I was before my brutal attack on April 20, 1998. In fact, I proudly admit that I have become a better person. I now see life from a different perspective. Family and friends are now more precious to me. I also see myself as a woman of strength and courage.

A random home invasion in an upscale neighborhood took the life of my husband of twenty-five years on that spring day in Newark, Delaware. We had only been in our home ten months when a crack cocaine addict, Donald Flagg, decided that he wanted to rape and kidnap a woman. With a gun and rope in his car, he set out to commit what he would later call the "perfect crime." He picked me, as I planted rose bushes in my front yard. When my husband, Nino, came home, he was shot and killed by the intruder. Upon entering our home, I was then attacked, raped and abducted by Nino's murderer. Fortunately, our 19-year-old twins, Melissa and Michael, were away at college. I was taken to my rapist's home, where I remained for five days. While bound and gagged, I was repeatedly raped with little hope of being rescued.

By the Grace of God, my determination to get back to my children — who were planning the funeral of their father — enabled me to draw upon my courage from within. It still amazes me that I was capable of surviving under such circumstances. During my captivity, I learned from the news media that law enforcement had no clues of my whereabouts, reporting that finding Debra Puglisi was like "looking for a needle in a haystack." I also had to read how my name had been entered into a national crime database as a suspect in my husband's murder! How could this be happening? My rapist was proud. When Flagg decided to discard the drugs from his home, I noticed a change in his demeanor. I could talk to him and, at times, he would release my ties. My instinct was to befriend him, to make him feel as though we were friends. During the rapes, I no longer fought him, holding back my tears of shame. It was like I dissociated, and he was raping my body...not my soul. By day four, he actually asked if I would like to have sex with him. I felt that saying yes would perhaps save my life. Probably the most humiliating, dehumanizing act was when my rapist insisted that he wash my hair. So intimate an act, having his hands massaging my scalp. As my husband's body was being prepared for burial, I was being groomed and raped by his murderer. I kept telling myself that these gruesome acts were necessary in order to survive.

By the fifth day, I had convinced this monster that we were friends. He changed the ropes that he had bound my wrists and ankles with to handcuffs. On the final day of my captivity, he went to work. I made the decision to try to escape. All odds were against me. However, I took the chance of getting to a landline phone and calling 911.

Within nine minutes, law enforcement was breaking down the door. I remained huddled against a wall, wrists and ankles cuffed. An ambulance was called and the news media instantly got word that Debra Puglisi was alive! Before I reached the local emergency room, programs across the nation were interrupted with the news that I had been rescued.

Returning to life with my children was bittersweet. I was alive, but my husband was gone. I had physical, emotional and spiritual wounds, as well as a criminal trial to prepare for. I had survivor's guilt, as well as the complicated grief of losing my husband and recovering from a horrific crime. I had the loving support of family, friends, and co-workers. In mid-May, I began treatment with my psychologist Dr. Constance Dancu. Of course, within one month of therapy, I was diagnosed with Post Traumatic Stress Disorder. Dr. Dancu provided me with the tools I needed to survive.

Survivor's guilt overwhelmed me, as I was the intended victim. I also had to learn that I was not damaged goods. The chosen mode of treatment was cognitive behavioral therapy. I had to make audiotapes, detailing the events of my victimization. As I listened, I would rate my feelings on a scale from one to five, with five meaning total despair. I was forced to undergo exposure therapy: looking at the perpetrator's picture. For weeks I was unable to look at his face without feeling pain, fear and anger. The most difficult task was saying his name. To this day, I still refer to him as "the asshole." After telling Dr. Dancu that I felt no man would ever want me, I learned to love myself and believe that I was worth being loved in return. I refer to this time as my "journey of healing." It was difficult, but soon I was convinced that my courage and strength to survive would empower me to become a true survivor.

In June, my children Melissa and Michael joined me at the Jersey shore where we moved in (cats too) with my Dad and Stepmom. One day a week, I would return to Delaware with either my Dad or brother Robert. Sometimes the drive was made in complete silence. I had doctors' appointments, physical therapy, sessions with the State Prosecutor, and mental health counseling. Having suffered forty-two physical injuries, I was left with gruesome scars on both wrists, bruising, ligature marks on my legs and ankles, as well as a broken toe. For about five weeks, I was an outpatient at a pain clinic where I received injections in my cervical spine to ease the nerve pain in my left wrist.

My family members were co-victims. Their pain was palpable. The community also grieved our loss, thoughtfully sending cards to remind us of their love and support. I will be forever grateful for the kindness showered upon Melissa, Michael, and me.

In the fall, I returned to the scene of the crime — my home. Against the wishes of my family, I moved back until I had to sell our home. All of the criminal evidence had been retrieved. I reclaimed my position as an on-call hospice nurse. The love and support of my co-workers was overwhelming. Law enforcement offered to escort me to neighborhoods that made me uncomfortable, and co-workers volunteered to help me regain confidence as I traveled across the county to care for the terminally ill.

Late in October, I became very upset about a legal matter related to the criminal trial. At Nino's viewing, an old boyfriend had offered support if I needed it. I found myself driving to his business, bursting into tears when I saw him. He locked the door and drove me to a quiet pub nearby. For one and one-half hours, Bill Sharp listened to me. He allowed me to purge my pain. I felt comfortable with Bill, having cared for him as a 19-year-old, lovesick teenager. Our relationship barely lasted one year back in 1970.

Bill continued to provide me with support and persuaded me to go out to social events. He made me feel safe. I fell in love with him all over again. Even Dr. Dancu gave us her blessings, as some would comment on how soon I kept company with another man. On July 21, 2000, we were married on the beach at the Jersey shore in the presence of family. Our wedding rings are inscribed "new beginnings."

Donald Flagg had been arrested as he worked on the assembly line at a Chrysler Plant. He immediately confessed that he was looking for a woman to kidnap and rape that afternoon in April. One year later, in April 1999, a death penalty case began. After five weeks of testimony during State v. Flagg, a jury voted seven to five for life in prison, without parole. Flagg received eight life sentences, plus 166 years. Several weeks later, the same Judge gave Flagg two additional life sentences for a rape that he committed just three days before my victimization. He will never hurt another woman.

In April 2000, I was asked to be a keynote speaker at a Victim's Rights Conference in Atlantic City, New Jersey. After sharing my message of hope, I was told that my story was inspirational. I have been invited by various groups in law enforcement, mental health, victim services and universities to share how I survived such a heinous crime. I am always amazed at the number of victims who approach me after my lectures to share their own story of victimization. No matter where I speak, other victims of sexual assault, homicide, incest and domestic violence are compelled to disclose their pain. It has been a rewarding experience to be a facilitator in assisting other victims to achieve their own physical, emotional and spiritual healing.

My book, *Shattered: Reclaiming A Life Torn Apart By Violence*, was published in August 2003, written in memory of Nino, the silent victim, and Dr. Dancu, who gave me the courage to live as a survivor. Writing my book was therapeutic. Shattered has become required reading in many universities, especially in the criminal justice curriculum. I truly believe that any victim service provider should listen to victims tell their stories. Too much emphasis has been placed on offenders in our judicial system. What about the effects of crime on victims and their families?

I have met wonderful people over the past fourteen years since my husband's death. God has truly placed me on a path of spiritual healing. As I travel across the country, I meet victims who need to be empowered to regain control of their lives. I thank God that He has chosen me to be part of the healing process of souls who deserve to be saved. As a Hospice nurse for sixteen years, I believe that teamwork is the best approach. Together, I believe the women in The Faces Behind the Pages that Inspire will achieve a common goal. We will go forth and share our inspirational stories.

Debra Puglisi Sharp is a Registered Nurse, Author and Inspirational Speaker. She has appeared on *Oprah, 20/20, Montel, The Bonnie Hunt Show, The John Walsh Show, Biography* on A&E, and most recently *Discovery*

Health. Her book, *Shattered: Reclaiming A Life Torn Apart By Violence,* was published in 2003. Debra served on the 911 Enhancement Board in Delaware. She now serves on the Board of Directors of the National Coalition of Victims in Action and is Co-Chair of the Sexual Assault Network of Delaware. On April 20, 2007, Debra was presented with the United States Attorney General's Special Courage Award through the Office for Victims of Crime in Washington, D.C.

    Personal Page: *http://www.facebook.com/DebraPuglisiSharp*
    Book Page: *http://www.facebook.com/Shattered:ReclaimingALifeTorn ApartByViolence*
    Web Site: *http://www.puglisisharp.com*
    Email: *Deb90333@aol.com*
    Linked In: *http://www.linkedin.com/in/DebraPuglisiSharp*

Meet Allison Sara of *Walking My Talk*

GREETINGS TO ALL who are reading this, because if you are, it means that you are on your path to enlightenment, by connecting your mind and body to the passion of your soul. By taking responsibility for changing your life and begin living your Dream. By becoming the best possible version of you. From Victim to "Victorious." Become a "Thriver" instead of a Survivor. It's time to become the bright shining star that you were born to be, to be the light to guide others from their darkness.

ALL IS LOVE . . . this journey is a walk back to ourselves to become one connected energy of unconditional LOVE with all. Imagine the sea as love and a portion is within each of our bodies. Although we all contain the same energy, we each have a different form, which makes us all unique and able to create our own separate adventures in this wonderful home we call Earth, to experience LIFE and to WALK OUR DREAMS.

FREEDOM is as close as your next choice.

There has never been such a time as this on earth before. The massive shift in consciousness is directed toward all who wish to awaken and become united as one. We must all take responsibility for our own actions and re-actions. What we give out, we must receive. There is no other way. We run our own debit and credits, so we can no longer blame anyone else for what we attract into our lives. It's time to let go of fear and embrace Life as the beautiful souls we truly are.

This is an adventure, not a survival test. Somewhere along the way, the messages changed and we began doubting ourselves and began trying to prove our worth. The darkness of Fear set in and we became lost. If we start each day with gratitude, anticipation and excitement, instead of dread and gloom, our journey will become a joyful one. If we choose to be happy, we will enjoy every experience from a place of gratitude. What we think becomes our reality.

Become a star and make a difference. Changes in our world can be achieved if we all work together. As each of us regains our inner-connected power, the light will increase. Never underestimate the power you personally can bring to the world. Let go of your past and fly. The most empowering thing we can do is to own that we, individually, have the power to change our experience of life from a negative one to a positive one — by choice. Change your thoughts and change your life. We cannot change others, but as we change, others around us will, as we lead by example.

There may never be a time when there is total Peace in our world. We must experience the darkness before we can become the light. We cannot experience the beauty that surrounds us without experiencing the ugliness, as well. The opposites — up / down, hot / cold, light / dark — will always co-exist. When we are filled with fear, we are fearful. Only by letting go of our fears can we fill the space within with Love. Ask and you shall receive, and the more you are grateful for, the more you receive to be grateful for — and the more you can share. The more worry and fear that we send to our problems, the worse they become. Worry is like praying in the negative.

The journey is ALL about self-worth and learning to love ourselves as one with all. It's not a selfish love, but one of caring and sharing from deep within our soul. We create Hell for ourselves, with failed relationships and marriages, illness, depression, addictions and total lack of self-worth, when we could have been creating Heaven. Being a Victim becomes our comfort zone, and at times we can see no way out of our continual circle of re-creating misery and despair, not only for ourselves, but as an example for our children.

By being at peace within — and truly owning that — we attract everything into our lives with our energy levels, making it easier to accept everyone and everything. Each of us is walking forward at our own pace, in our own way. There is no "one size fits all" path. There are many, but they all lead to ONENESS.

No one can make us happy, or hurt. How we choose to feel towards any situation is our own choice. We all experience feelings of anger and pain during our life, with illness, death, depression, addiction and loneliness. It takes as much energy to be miserable as it does to be happy, and while you are focusing on one, there is no space left for the other. We cannot be positive and negative at the same time. We cannot avoid pain, but we can rise above it with acceptance, faith and love. Peace within starts when we own that we are NOT our bodies; we are a powerful energy of love linked to all. If we damage another in any way, we are also damaging a part of ourselves. If we choose to be happy, and spread joy and happiness, we will create miracles — not only within ourselves, but also for others, by example.

Life is about constant change. We are not the person we were yesterday, but it is the experience we gained in all our yesterdays that has created the person we are today. The sooner we own gratitude as our way forward in each moment, the better our lives become.

Fear is False Evidence Appearing Real, and our old habits and illusions have become so real to us that we are unable to stand back and see the "Big Picture." We are totally in control of our own lives, and there is no one coming to rescue us. We have the power as individuals to take a stand, to own who we are, and to begin "consciously" giving to others what we would like to receive ourselves. To be Love ~ not just give it, but to BE IT, with total acceptance of all in our hearts.

You can start today. There is no waiting period. If you are holding your breath "waiting for life" to happen, you can start breathing NOW — your life has arrived! It's yours to "create" any time you choose. Start each day with a blank sheet; the story you write is up to you. Remember this: whatever you give power to with your thoughts becomes your reality. It must be so if you focus your energy on it. Positive thoughts create positive results, and negative thoughts create negative outcomes — always.

G.O.D ~ Gratitude Opens Doors. Gratitude and acceptance are the most important tools to nurture within yourself. Acceptance of yourself and others, no matter what, is the closest vibrational energy to Love we will attain as a human. We are a Soul within a body, having a human experience, to finally accept that we are NOT separate, but connected to all within the universe.

Facebook is an amazing social networking tool that allows us to share wisdom and love with all those looking for inspiration and a better way for all to live. If you wish to be inspired, then inspire others. If you wish to be loved, love others.

I started my page, *Walking My Talk [www.facebook.com/ IamWalkingmyTalk]* in April 2012, and I was amazed at all the new inspirational pages that appeared as if by magic around the same time, like a gigantic tidal wave sweeping the world with love, wisdom, compassion, sharing, inspiration and hope. There is a wonderful, supportive energy between the different pages. Many of us are saying the same things in a slightly different way, and everyone is happy to share, just as long as the messages get "out there."

HOW you live your life is Your Choice. At any moment, you can choose to stop yourself when you feel you are "over-reacting" to old habits. Your mind is a very powerful tool, and combined with your soul and your body, the journey can be lived in harmony...if you choose it. Most humans have their ego placed firmly in the driver's seat, while their soul waits patiently in the back seat for the time to awaken. All three — Mind, Body and Soul — must play together in harmony for us to lead a balanced, happy and rewarding life.

The world is out of balance. This is where YOU can play your part. Look back long enough to forgive and forget any pain you have experienced on this journey. The people who caused the pain are other souls finding their own way, lashing out with blame and confusion to deal with their own inner fears. When we accept that we are one, it is easier to understand the actions of others, knowing that their actions were not intended to "hurt us," but to fill a need within "them" to deal with their own fears of insecurity, scarcity and loneliness. Many use addictions to fill the emptiness within or to run away from their "perceived" reality.

The ones that we believe have hurt us are the ones we learn the most from, once we understand the reason they are part of our drama. When we accept that we are one, there is no longer any feeling of separation. We can accept that whatever others do or say is "their" truth as a human. We can understand that there is no longer any need for judgment, allowing free will to play its part.

We truly make our lives Heaven or Hell by our personal choices, responses or reactions from the past. Set yourself FREE. Allowing others to be free, without control or manipulation, will change your life in miraculous ways. Our bodies may age, but our hearts can stay as young as we feel within. Our soul never ages or dies; it just changes form. Why not be Young at Heart forever? Shine your light brightly each day to embrace all with the warmth of your smile and your Love. Make your life one of caring and sharing.

Our dreams are always within our capabilities to fulfill. We all have different skills and dreams, but we are all united in wanting to change the world together. It is — and always will be — a team effort. Be happy, be colorful, be positive and play your part in making a difference and helping the world to be a better place by focusing on Love.

The time is NOW! Stop trying to change others, cast off your disease and BE the changes as a guiding Star of love, inspiration and compassion.

Let your life be the example of Love and WALK YOUR DREAM. Love changes ME to WE.

Allison Sarah's Facebook page is *Walking My Talk [www.facebook.com/IamWalkingmyTalk]*, where she shares inspiration, love, hope, faith, wisdom, beauty and guidance to all souls wishing to unite with LOVE. Her life has been a series of ups and downs, as she learnt and grew towards ONENESS with all. Her dream is to "Make a Difference" and the skills she needs to create this Dream are as natural to her as breathing. She's an artist, teacher/student and a writer. She is sharing wisdom with All in these wondrous times on earth. Change ME to WE in the Name of LOVE. All 1 Son

http://facebook.com/all1sonSara
https://facewbook.com/IamWalkingmyTalk

Meet Michele Penn of *Peace in the Present Moment*

My book with Eckhart Tolle, *Peace in the Present Moment*, is the result of my journey to consciousness. I created my Facebook page, *Peace in the Present Moment,* out of a desire to tell my story, provide inspiration, ideas, books, quotes and even exquisite floral furniture to aid in your awakening. I want to share love and contribute to raising your consciousness and vibration. Through my personal story, you can learn how to manifest your dreams. I want to aid you in living the magnificently happy and fulfilling life that you deserve. Whatever I can do to put you in that feel good place.

My ex-husband verbally abused my children and me for years. He eventually threatened to kill me in an emotionally violent rage. I can forgive him today, because that experience was the catalyst that fueled my desire for spiritual knowledge. I left him, and instead of losing my life, I found it. I heard Oprah say, "Forgiveness is letting go of the hope that the past could be any different." And, by forgiving myself, I was set free. I discovered a strength in myself. I was on a new path.

I became aware of flowers after I truly forgave the unforgivable. Where had they been my whole life? Why had I not seen them before? I was being awakened to their beauty by my ability to forgive. I was captivated by their inner beauty, the soul of the flower, and had an intense desire to capture that moment for others. There is where I felt joy and peace. There is where I lost myself in oneness with nature. Flowers are astonishing. Nature is magnificent. I didn't know yet what this incredibly peaceful feeling was. I later discovered it was presence — and I was becoming awakened.

I was given Eckhart Tolle's book, *The Power of Now*, and it changed my life. I learned to let go of the past and live in the now. In the present, all negativity dissolves. Reading Eckhart's next book, *A New Earth*, intensified the process of awakening for me. The first chapter was called "The Flowering of Human Consciousness," and while I was reading it, I felt as if Eckhart was in my head. He touched my soul with his words. I had never been touched by words before in this way. He wrote why I was drawn to taking photographs of flowers!

Wow!

Eckhart says, "seeing beauty in a flower could awaken humans, however briefly, to the beauty that is an essential part of their own innermost being, their true nature." Flowers AWAKENED ME. I was awakened to something so real and still. I was conscious without thought. I had the spiritual awakening that Eckhart wrote about when I captured the moment of beauty in a flower. Eckhart says "flowers are a window for you into the formless." I felt that deep within my soul.

Wow!

A flower could do that? Flowers awakened me? Yes. I felt true joy, peace and happiness, and I began to realize that they come from within. I was In The Present Moment and loving it. Eckhart says, "You are never more essentially, more deeply, yourself than when you are still."

I then had an inspired thought. Oprah always says to believe that thought and act upon it. I KNEW that Eckhart would connect with my flowers as profoundly as I connected with his words, because they are a representation of exactly what he talked about. I connected with his words so well that chills still run through my body when I think of it. When Eckhart said he was "increasingly drawn to and fascinated by flowers," I knew exactly how he felt. They provided me with such inspiration. So, I decided to design a mock-up book, with my photos and his quotes from *A New Earth*. I didn't know how it was going to happen, but I KNEW we were going to do a book together. I kept my vibration high. I believed and never questioned it again. I knew it was DONE — and I was going to enjoy the journey. I began to feel the feelings of what it's like to have this book on the shelves of

Barnes and Noble or the pages of Amazon. I wasn't pretending, I was FEELING as if it were already true. I lived as if it were true. Everyone told me it was a crazy dream. Why would Eckhart want to do a book with you? But, I didn't listen to anything outside of myself. I was vibrating so high from this inner knowing. Eckhart taught me this. I had this incredible passion to create a way for people to read Eckhart's words and meditate on my flowers in one place. It was brilliant — and nobody ever thought of it. I didn't know how it was going to happen, but I knew the universe would make a way. So the story unfolds.

I was at a Louise Hay conference in Tampa, Florida, and exhibition booths lined the hallway selling all kinds of spiritual products. I went up to a table and looked at beautiful candles that stood 16" high by 12" wide. I ordered a candle and had it shipped. Weeks later when it arrived, it came in the wrong color. So, I called Lori Rekowski, the woman who sold it to me, and left her a message. She called me back and said "things always happen for a reason." I believe that, too, but I couldn't imagine what this reason could be.

I was sure it would be exciting. We continued to talk on the phone about our lives and our spiritual journey. I spoke of my intention with Eckhart Tolle and my flowers (she had already seen my notecards with my flower photos on them.) She told me that she had written a powerful book called A Victim No More and that her publisher had just done a children's book with Eckhart. She was so inspired by my photos — and my story — that she said she would contact her publisher for me and see if he would listen to my idea.

Days later, she told me that I was given permission to e-mail some photos and my idea to the publisher. She informed me that I should be short and sweet, because he was doing this as a favor to her. He apparently had manuscripts from floor to ceiling to review for this month alone. So, I did just that. I actually heard back from the publisher — Bob Friedman of Hampton Roads Publishing — pretty quickly. He loved it and said it was a great idea, but, he didn't think we could get Eckhart to agree. Bob said he would gladly connect me with other spiritual authors, but I reminded Bob that my inspiration, vision, dreams and passion was the connection with Eckhart Tolle. And then I told him that I KNEW if we could get Eckhart to look at my work, he would feel the same inspiration and passion that I did. Bob asked for a mock-up of my book. Instead, I asked if I could fly up and meet with him in person so I could see his face when he opened the book.

After Bob Friedman met with me, he called in the CEO and marketing director, and they loved it, too. Again, they reiterated that it was a LONG SHOT to get Eckhart to even look at this idea. Because I seemed determined and inspired, they said they would send it to Eckhart's publisher, Namaste, in Canada. Weeks went by. Months went by. I continued to feel the feelings as if it were DONE. I didn't once question whether Eckhart would get to see it, or whether he would like it, because I KNEW. I received the phone call from Bob Friedman, the Hampton Roads publisher, and he said, "I am in shock, but because of your genuine spirit, passion and belief, we are on second base. Namaste loves it and has agreed to show it to Eckhart Tolle." I knew it. As the months went by, I never got discouraged because news wasn't coming quickly enough. It didn't matter to me how long it took, because I knew it was done. I allowed myself to enjoy the JOURNEY. After some time, I received the phone call confirming that Eckhart loved it, too! He said he wanted to do the book with me! I KNEW it.

I didn't feel differently at all when I heard the news, because I was already vibrating so high in the knowing that it was DONE. On the other hand, my friends and family were so surprised and impressed. They couldn't believe that I could manifest something like that. We can all make our dreams come true if we just believe in the power. So, we were on our way. Eckhart wanted to include Byron Katie in the book, as well, because their teachings are so similar and they have never collaborated before. I also love Byron Katie's work, especially her book A Thousand Names for Joy. How exciting! I signed a contract and the book was due out later that year. Four months later, I received a phone call from the CEO of Hampton Roads, telling me that they decided not to print the book.

Because of the economy, it wasn't feasible anymore to print a full-color book, so they were canceling our contract. When I got off the phone, I didn't get upset. I knew this was just part of the journey, because the book is already DONE. With my belief in tow, I called the CEO back a few days later and had an incredible, positive conversation. I talked about how the world needed to be inspired by this great combination of quotes and flowers. I talked from my heart and soul. And then, he agreed. So, we were back on track. We renegotiated the contract. It's all just part of the journey. *Peace in the Present Moment* was published October 2010.

I continue to manifest amazing things into my life. I attracted the man of my dreams by using the law of attraction and the power of the present moment. I am living the life I always imagined.

 In *Peace in the Present Moment,* Michele Penn's breathtaking floral photographs add color, peace and a deep stillness to the wisdom of Eckhart Tolle and Byron Katie. Michele's "soul shots" are a symbol of enlightenment. She was raised in Short Hills, New Jersey, attended Millburn High School and graduated with a bachelor's degree from Syracuse University in 1982. Her three beautiful children, Freddy, Nicole and Melanie, fill her life with inspiration. Michele lives in Sarasota, Florida, with David, the man of her dreams. As an award-winning photographer, a wonderful speaker, a woman who owns her own business — *CreativeElegancebyMichele.com* — she wants to enrich other people's lives by sharing the love behind her Facebook page at:

http://www.facebook.com/peaceinthepresentmoment

Also, visit

www.PeaceInThePresentMoment.net
www.CreativeEleganceByMichele.com

Meet Dr. Charles F. Glassman of *Coach MD*

WHY WOULD A LOCAL doc from a small county just north of New York City start a Facebook page that now attracts fans from all over the world?

About five years ago, a patient came into my office. As he had during most of his visits, this patient expressed enormous gratitude for the time I spent with him and the knowledge that I imparted. That's what I do. It has always been hard for me to zip in and zip out, grabbing my prescription pad along the way, fleeing into the next room — the dynamic of modern medicine. So, I changed my practice a number of years ago to allow more time with each patient. But life goes on outside my office — and even though this man, let me call him Larry, appreciated my time, information and guidance, there was a problem. Larry said that he felt great afterward each visit, fully motivated and charged up, but then he would return to his life, chock full of responsibilities and stresses, and things would fall apart, rather quickly. He asked if there was a way I could keep him motivated between office visits.

We decided that on each Monday, I would send him an email message. That message had much more of a motivational or inspirational tone, rather than medical. A few weeks went by, and I realized this message could apply to more people than just Larry. So I accumulated the email addresses of my patients and others, and each week they would get my message. That was the birth of my "Weekly Message." As the weeks went on, my messages became longer. Writing every week was challenging, but eventually I found it to be necessary, not only for my patients, but for me. It became a personal therapy as I'd look into myself and explore what it was that would sabotage me or cause me to become unmotivated. What were the things that caused me to feel down? Angry? Passive? Aggressive? Sick? And not only did I look into myself, but I began pulling in contemporary topics and would weigh in on those and how they might affect the way we feel.

The more I wrote, the more people would tell me I should turn my weekly messages into a book. This process started around the time when The Secret book and DVD was becoming popular. The same people would tell me that my writing reminded them of concepts shared in that book. With their encouragement, I watched the DVD and later read the book. Then I realized that, indeed, much of the motivational, inspirational and practical guidance I delivered through my message had similarities to the basic concept of this work. However, I felt I still had a lot more to learn and clarify before writing a book of my own.

About six months into writing messages every week, I teamed up with a nutritionist with the idea of starting a corporate consulting business. I would provide the "medical" stress management/relaxation piece, she would provide the nutritional advice piece, and we would hire someone to teach practical exercise at the workplace. This felt like a great idea, so we built the program during the better part of ten months. All along, I continued writing my messages every week (and maintained my medical practice, of course). Ten months later, on a Saturday morning in May 2008, I received a call from my partner in this business. Her voice was quieter and more guarded than usual. She explained that she could not continue the business due to personal reasons. Suddenly my plans and visions, and a lot of hard work, appeared to be washed down the drain. Not to mention the fact that I had committed to a new home renovation with the vision that, with this new business, we could easily afford the added expense. Now, it appeared to be a large albatross. For an hour or so, I felt pretty deflated. I showered and went into my meditation. I had meditated on and off again for many years. As I got deep into this particularly long meditation, my inner guidance spoke to me loudly and clearly with three directions: "meditate every day; you don't need anybody but yourself; and turn your weekly messages into a book."

That Monday, instead of distributing my usual "Weekly Message," I shared the first installment of my book (yet to be named). The next day, one of my patients came to the office, installment in hand, with many red marks on it. He explained that he was a retired editor from Consumer Reports magazine and that all "great" writers need an editor. Putting me in this group was shameless flattery! His editing was terrific and I retained him on the spot. For the next 20 weeks, I would deliver him a chapter prior to distributing it to my email list. And after 20 weeks, I had a 19-chapter book manuscript. I also engaged my audience to name the book. The working title was Ego to Essence. I submitted the manuscript to agent Bill Gladstone, who represented author Eckhart Tolle. Our paths had crossed a few years earlier when I had written several chapters for another author he represented. Bill took the project, only to pass it off to assistants and — in an aloof relationship — his agency dropped me a few months later. I received that notice by email while watching my son's 9th grade orchestra performance. They said my platform was not large enough and they wished me luck.

Back to square one, it seemed. A few months passed and I decided to work on a proposal to resubmit my book to agents and/or publishers. A woman with a local radio show heard about me, and after speaking with me on the phone, she came to my office and asked me to appear on her show. She said, "What are you wasting your time with agents or publishers? Why don't you just do it yourself?" I remembered the words from my inner guidance, "You don't need anybody but yourself." I interpreted this to mean that I needed to take responsibility and take the lead in representing myself — by using my gifts and talents — and not delegate that to someone else or hide behind someone else's direction. One morning, about a month before I met this woman, the name of the book popped into my head: Brain Drain.

I took her advice and, with her help, got down to business. I chose a graphic designer to create the book, and I selected an Israeli printer. In

November 2009, the first printed books arrived from Israel! In December 2009, I attended a weekend event, "Movers and Shakers," put on by Reid Tracy, CEO of Hay House, and Cheryl Richardson, author and one of the Hay House celebrities. On Saturday, they announced that we'd be working on public speaking the following day, Sunday. I knew they were going to pick a couple people from the audience (of about 170 participants) to use as examples. That Saturday evening, while out with my wife and friends, I explained how there was no way I would parade myself in front of everybody to be ripped apart in the name of education. However, when I awoke that morning, I asked myself, "Don't I want to be recognized by Hay House? If it wasn't for my nerves, wouldn't I do what it takes to do that?" I decided that I would make sure I was among those to be picked.

I arrived early and positioned myself in front of the empty room to familiarize myself with the space. I anticipated that Reid Tracy would arrive through the back door before the conference started. As I paced in the front of the room, I stabilized my hands from shaking, holding a warm cup of tea. When he walked through the door, I slowly approached him, introduced myself, and said, "I would like to be the first speaker today." We spoke for a few minutes, and he perused a copy of my book briefly, expressing his surprise that I did the self-publishing. As the conference started, they did indeed call me up. To my surprise, Louise Hay was in the front row. What was supposed to be a five to ten-minute speech turned into twenty-five, as both Reid and Cheryl encouraged me to continue. Very little criticism came my way. The warmth, love and incredible feedback I received from the audience was awe-inspiring. After that event, Reid and I exchanged emails for a few months. In the final email, he asked me to check in with him again when my platform (audience) was bigger. After all, how many books could they expect to sell from a local doc who practices in a small county just north of New York City? And who would want to listen to him?

During the past two years, my book Brain Drain has won many independent publishing awards, from self-help to spirituality. Soon after the final email from Reid Tracy, I thought long and hard about what it is that I do. With my book and weekly messages, I was seeing more and more patients seeking guidance and coaching rather than purely medical advice, treatment or diagnosis. After listening to a webinar about how to brand yourself, a light bulb flashed: I am a coach. I am an M.D. I am Coach MD!

Knowing that my mission to get mind, body, and spirit working as one unit was so successful in my small practice, I began to realize my true, life purpose. It became clear that my message is a universal one, and the more people I could reach, the more I could help, and the more I would be a doctor in the most authentic form of the word.

With the explosion of social media and the ability it has to bring people together, I felt that there was no better vehicle than Facebook to begin my career as a doctor. Certainly, this may sound odd to those who know that my career began more than twenty years ago. But this new career, as Coach MD, is special, focusing on the reality that it is our common, everyday challenges that get us sick or keep us sick. It takes constant reinforcement and daily practice and reminders to keep us on the right track. What began with a "Weekly Message" has evolved into daily Facebook reminders — shared with a much larger audience.

Growing my Facebook page was not done totally by word of mouth. I advertise on Facebook. Having watched and read The Secret, I knew that followers of that book and video could not possibly be getting the results that were promised. How could I know that? Because I was just like everybody else — and I knew what happened when things start going well in my life. Suddenly (uncontrollably and automatically), thoughts pop in my mind to prepare me for the next shoe to drop. Through my book and weekly message, I've worked through that, and now I wanted to help others achieve what I had — and make the law of attraction work for them. I decided to target/market Facebook followers of The Secret. These people didn't know me, so marketing was essential to introduce me to them. I began attracting people to my online site and continue to do so, both organically and through some advertising.

Positive comments I get from all over the world make it quite clear that my decision to touch people through the technological world of social media has been a great decision. It has also reaffirmed this to me: We all possess certain human traits and characteristics that can either help us thrive or cause us to struggle. Through Facebook, I have begun to help more and more people thrive. With the development of my other programs, systems and future books, I know that as Coach MD, I will be in a position to help many others. My journey has been an interesting one, and it is just beginning. At the time this book's printing, I have more than 20,000 followers from 20 different countries, and my followers are growing at a rate of between two to four thousand fans a month. Just think, when I began my weekly message and started my book, I'd never heard of Facebook. I can hardly believe that the "platform" that people in the publishing industry told me I needed is growing right before my eyes, because of Facebook! With this growth, I am confident that my desire to become the doctor of my dreams will come to fruition — and my contribution will leave the world a slightly better place. I thank Facebook for providing me the opportunity for this leg of my journey.

 Charles F. Glassman, M.D., FACP, has practiced general internal medicine for more than 20 years. Dr. Glassman is the author of the critically acclaimed book Brain Drain, winner of many awards including the 2011 Independent Publisher's Award and 2011 Eric Hoffer Award as the best Self-Help and Health book. In 2010, Dr. Glassman began blending his caring as a medical doctor with the passion and guidance of a life coach. He is now known as Coach MD — a transformational approach to healthcare; turning sickness into health by showing people how mind, body and spirit can work as one unit. Dr. Glassman has appeared on ABC news, Bloomberg Radio, NPR, Sirius/XM, Hay House Radio, The Wall Street Journal Radio, and numerous others around the country speaking on his unique approach to health care. He lives in Rockland County, New York, with his wife and four children.

www.TheCoachMD.com
www.Facebook.com/CoachMD
www.youtube.com/CharlesGlassmanMD
www.CharlesGlassmanMDblog.com
www.webtalkradio.net/shows/medicine-on-the-cutting-edge

Meet Tammy Plunkett and Charlene Winchester Of *The Bridge Post*

THERE ARE VERY MANY times in our lives where we think we want something only to have the powers-that-be give us something else. More often than not, that something else is more precious and divine than anything we could have asked for. It is quite realistic, however, that as human beings we can never be conscious of all that is available to us. So we have to trust and have faith that if we don't get what we want, we'll at least get what we need.

This is the lesson we share with you.

The Bridge Post was conceived by Charlene Winchester, a stay-at-home, mother of three, who saw a need to reconnect families. She felt that, with the age of smartphones and tablets fully upon us, we risk alienating family members. But instead of fighting the new technology as so many of our historical predecessors have fought change to no avail, she envisioned using it to bridge the gap in families. I now have to ask myself if this perceived need wasn't also her subconscious pointing out something missing in her own family life.

I am Tammy Plunkett, a work-from-home mother of four. Charlene overheard me talking about my writing with some moms at the school-yard gate and approached me about writing for The Bridge Post, which at the time was still an idea and not even a webpage. Little did either of us know that this first encounter would be the birth of a loving friend-ship and successful business partnership.

At the time, I was re-launching a holistic health business and strug-gling with trying to identify health issues in my oldest daughter, but for some reason The Bridge Post spoke to me. I didn't think I had the time, and I feared I didn't have enough publishing experience, and as Charlene's vision got clearer and larger I also came to the realization that I would have to drop my healing practice. Despite it all, I decided to trust what the universe was sending to me and let my intuition guide me towards Charlene's vision.

By the time we saw a lawyer about a partnership agreement for BusyWoman Productions, and met with a web-designer for The Bridge Post, I learned that the cause of my fifteen-year-old daughter's failing health was an addiction to drugs. I come from a long line of addicts and alcoholics, and I have more experience with addiction than I have ever cared to have, so if it's true that children choose their parents, my daugh-ter chose wisely. Not to say it is a walk in the park, because it's far from it. Being in the present moment, and not taking what she says personally, and deciding to let her learn from her mistakes on her own journey are mantras I have to repeat many times a day. But I also know that this drug addiction is not the true being of my daughter. I love that true being unconditionally, and I hold firm to the belief that she will come out of this a more enlightened being.

In the midst of all those hardships, we created The Bridge Post. Our mission statement claimed it was an interactive web-magazine where we give every member of the family a voice, and all opinions get equal airtime. Industry professional articles are published alongside use-gen-erated content in the form of blogs and multimedia posts with the goal that all this rich content will give family members something to talk about in person. We launched while Charlene and I were away at a con-ference learning to develop games and apps which we could incorporate into our website to increase family connectedness. We had big goals and we were going to transform families for the better. And because we all know that the core of any media strategy today is social media, we began a Facebook fan page to drive traffic to our main site.

What we got, however, was something life changing.

As we began to share memes, make our own original posters, and encourage conversation, we began to insert a piece of ourselves into the Facebook page. As administrators, we started to share our own life struggles, triumphs, and joys, finding in return an earnest friendship from our fans. We got back a conversation about their lives, and an appreciation for the ideas that we were passing on. Our marketing place soon transformed into a community sitting around a very large virtual kitchen table. Our fans dropped in and out regularly, and we came to know them as people, knowing whom our posts, would touch, and worrying when we didn't hear from them. In a nutshell, we found friendship, connectivity, learning, and support. We found the very things we hoped for, but what we didn't expect was that we would come to depend on our fans as much as they depended on us.

Charlene posts with her heart on the page, typically taking a cheerful but thought-provoking approach that she attributes to her appreciation for self-awareness. Dealing with a hangover resulting from years of sadness after her mother's unmourned death when Charlene was only five-years-old, she savors happiness in the simplicity of life. She has also taken-in and cares for her developmentally disabled sister. From those lessons she shares the meaning and inspiration behind achievement, compassion, and mindset. She posts as a mother whose goal is to empower families with a belief that understanding begins with listening, support is best given with thoughtful expression, and a team needs a common goal. She posts about her longing for her remote extended family and desire for connection with them.

She initially posted as a wife sharing an appreciation of the longevity of life, what it takes to be a friend and the reality that people change. And then reality did change—drastically.

Within a couple of weeks she got the one-two punch of finding a lump on her breast and her husband confirming disconnect in their marriage. The Bridge Post followers, and the wisdom in the posters we shared, were her anchor and her soft place to land. She is now using the outlet we offer to others and pours out her deepest feelings, getting validation and reassurance from others in return.

Understandably, The Bridge Post website got a little less attention as the families in both our lives came first. In the developmental stages, we were still conducting focus groups and getting feedback on any changes that were needed. Once Charlene got the clear of the C-word from a battery of tests, and both she and her husband were in marriage counseling, we sat down to review the scope and possibilities for The Bridge Post while bearing in mind everything we had going on in our respective families.

There is a term used a lot in entrepreneurial circles: pivot. It means to make a course correction within your established marketplace by altering a product offering or going after a different set of customers. We were facing such a pivot. Neither one of us could deny the inspiration that was being derived from The Bridge Post. Not only had we received a ton of feedback from our readers, users, and fans, but we ourselves had been inspired. Our mission statement had to change. We were no longer only about giving family members a voice; we were also about making individual family members whole. How much better can a family be if all of their members are coming from an authentic place of completeness?

And that brings us back to trusting what the universe hands to us. I asked for a thriving health and wellness consulting practice and sat waiting for the phone to ring; in return I got a whole community of people to inspire and be inspired from. Charlene wanted to help families become closer through the use of technology; she is still working towards that noble goal, she just uses a different map now. She is encouraging all of us to find our authentic, whole self while using technology to connect and empower the family. Our hardships have held lessons. We have pivoted. And we hope to help and inspire our followers as much as they have helped and inspired us.

 Tammy Plunkett started her career as a nurse, then studied and practiced alternative medicine. She has written and critiqued fiction for over ten years, winning an award in 2007. She is now the Executive Editor for *The Bridge Post,* while raising a family of four with her wonderful husband. Charlene Winchester left a career in business administration and communications to care for her three children and developmentally disabled sister. During this time she successfully owned and operated a small creative business before founding BusyWoman Productions. She lives in Ottawa, Canada with her husband and family.

http://www.facebook.com/thebridgepost
http://www.thebridgepost.com

Meet Necole Stephens
Spirit Medium, Bereaved Mom, Sibling and Daughter

I WAKE UP EVERY morning, drink my coffee and get my kids ready for school, usually with tears silently rolling down my cheek, knowing that I am making one breakfast too little. I do laundry, wash dishes, pay bills, discipline, watch my boys play football and live just like most everyone else but have the heartbeat of a grieving mom. What makes me different is this; not only am I a mom, wife, bereaved parent, bereaved sibling, and bereaved daughter. I am a Spirit Medium. I see "dead people" as everyone else calls it. I never call it that. I always refer to the "dead people" as our love ones. Our love ones that I am humbly honored to be able to connect with every day.

I don't have "special powers". I have been blessed with a gift, a gift that even I don't understand at times. I am sharing with you my story as a bereaved parent along with my many sleepless nights and as a Spirit Medium with what I know is to be true. I am traveling a painful journey similar to so many, yet also a journey of a different kind. I have one foot in both worlds. I call this living in "Duality". Even to me, this can be quite conflicting. I know of something greater nevertheless I want my baby back home with me. This is my story of how my Mediumship intertwines with the most horrifying tragedy of all...

My journey of healing started when I was just three years old and began to see Spirit. While asleep in bed one night, I was awaked by a man and had no idea who this was. Terrified, I ran into my parents room, screaming "There's a man in my room!" My parents being typical parents, insisted that I was dreaming and that I go back to my room.

I defiantly continued to scream "No! There is a man in my room!" so they caved and allowed me to sleep on the living room couch for several months. Over the next several years, bedtime became a battle for me. I starting "seeing things" again and would wake screaming or sleep walking and talking. Sometimes I would wake in a different part of my house with no idea how I got there. My mother became increasingly concerned and thought I was "going crazy". I quickly learned how to "turn this off".

I remember while visiting my nana, overhearing her speak to her friend. She told her "My mother will read your cards, go on upstairs." I asked her about this. What was she talking about? She explained that her and her mother "knew" things. They had what she referred to as premonitions. She continued to explain it was a gift they had, as well as a few other family members. I finally confided in her about me. She told me that what I was seeing and hearing was real but to keep it to myself or people would think I was strange. Being a child and trusting her, I did just that. During my high school years, I shared my experience with two of my best friends. We still talk about how different things were back then.

One thing my gift was not able to do for me is prevent tragedy from striking not just one time, but three times in three short years. I have and continue to struggle with the passing of my only sibling; my brother Stephen, my precious, healthy eleven-year-old son passing unexpectedly in his sleep twenty-two months later, and my father passing just a short nine months after my son. Being that I have been blessed with this amazing gift one would think I might have an opportunity to change the future, a "window" I like to call it, to change what the Universe had in store for me but even being a Medium, I am not exempt from that. The moment we bring a child into the world is when we realize our world is greater, our lives have meaning and that we want to be better people. We yearn to pause, hold on to and cherish the time for eternity. Little do we realize our hearts and memory have started a scrapbook of their own, and create an eternal treasure of memories that time and space could never erase.

Every day, I am reminded that the deepest things in life are intangible: love, wisdom, faith, doubt, fear, hope, beauty, and passion. These cannot be held in our hand, but they shape our life. Yet, we all still crave the tangible... There are the moments in your life that make you and set the course of who you're going to be. Sometimes they're little, subtle moments. Sometimes they're big moments you never saw coming.

No one asks for their life to change, but it does. It's what you do afterwards that counts. This is when you find out who you are and what you are capable of. This is the time when we see the true essence of our being. We each have a hunger to learn more, to see more...to know there is more. We are not alone as each of us struggles to open fully to life. Each of us is looking to know what this great mystery is all about.

We are searching for the answers, which we may not even be meant to know. It is then that those intangible words have to stand true... I began to fully pursue and "own" my Mediumship shortly after my brother passed, I knew he was my "gatekeeper" and together we would make a difference in people's lives. Ironically, I also began working with more bereaved families prior to becoming one myself.

I truly just want to help people, help people know that there is more than we we see and help them on their journey. Finding some type of healing and a bit of comfort, even if just for a few short moments. No one knows how you feel to have your child taken before his or her time; other than another mother. The feeling of connecting a family with their love one is an indescribable feeling; I can't put into words how it fills my soul. It has and continues to truly assist me, in my own healing.

I started working again just three months after the passing of my son, I read for over two hundred bereaved parents at no charge. I just felt the need to give as many people as possible the opportunity to connect and validation that their love one was okay and always around. I created my Facebook page, and currently writing a book in the hopes to inspire and help people with their grief or struggles. For people to know that they aren't alone, we are all on this painful journey together. I also believe that my Facebook page isn't only inspiring for people who are dealing with grief, but who could be dealing with other struggles in their lives as well. My goal is to try to help people know that there is more, there is a plan and that you can and will survive. It may not be easy, but some how, some way you will make it. We have already lived the worst day of our life and we made it through somehow, we are stronger than we believe possible.

I hope through my Facebook page, Blog, Newsletter and my future book, reading about my journey and inspirations will help others with what the future holds for them. Grief is a constant daily struggle that does not improve with time. It changes with time. We somehow become connected to our love in Spirits essence rather than the grief. Grasping on what is now becoming your new "normal" is the most difficult challenge and to know you are not alone can be so comforting. Everyone that I connect with becomes a special part of me, with the use of my gift; I will continue to bring a moment of peace to as many as I can. We are truly all in this together; in this crazy journey we call LIFE.

 Necole Stephens, New England Spirit Medium, nationally recognized, has dedicated her life to the helping and healing of others. Necole travels across the country delivering validating and evidential messages from love ones in Spirit during her "Angel Kisses" Group readings. Necole continues to offer private sessions and is currently working on her first book. Necole continues to inspire others daily through her Facebook Fan Page which she refers to as her "therapy". Necole is the founder of a non profit 501(c)3 organization in loving memory of her son, Zachary Tompkins. Zachary was a healthy, athletic 11 year old boy who passed unexpectedly in his sleep in March 2010.

www.facebook.com/NecoleStephens2
www.zacharytompkins.org

Meet Gail Alexander, *Energy Mandalas*

FROM WHAT I REMEMBER about my childhood, I always wanted to be outside, enjoying nature. I have always been connected to everything.

Between the ages of 4 and 6, however, I experienced a string of traumatic events. I had a lazy eye and wore an eye patch throughout first grade. When I had a tonsillectomy and adenoidectomy, I learned I could breathe and eat at the same time. My grandfather died of a massive heart attack several weeks after I told my parents he was going to die. I knew my mom had experienced a stillbirth before I was told. Even at this young age, I received the message loud and clear that no one wanted to know what I was going to say or do next — so I turned to food. I learned quickly that sugar — and constant eating — silenced the messages coming to me in my mind. I developed allergies to nature, so I could no longer go outside anymore and, therefore, felt as if I were no longer connected to everything. I learned to turn inwardly and began to take everything out on myself.

Grammar school and adolescence did not go so well, either. By this time, I was grossly overweight and had what counselors call "school refusal" issues. I didn't want to be there. My parents, worried about my weight and other concerns, took me to a variety of doctors and therapists; they finally had me see one of their friends who had become a therapist. That was a breakthrough for me, because it was the first time anyone had ever asked me how I felt and what I thought about what was going on around me. That relationship started to turn my life around. For the first time, I actually felt like someone wanted to hear what I had to say.

When it was time to go to college, I was completely unprepared for living on my own, for I had led a very sheltered life with little responsibility. However, I survived and learned to manage. I graduated from college and earned a master's degree in counseling.

After finishing graduate school, I had an allergic reaction to penicillin. It poisoned my entire body and I almost died. I was told it was going to take a long time to feel better — and the truth of the matter is, I never fully recovered from this illness. I continue to be allergic to many types of foods and drugs.

It was at this time in my life when my intuitive gifts — which I had tried to silence by stuffing them down or numbing them out — returned, albeit slowly, as I began to perceive when my loved ones were going to die. I also began receiving visitations and messages from relatives who had crossed over.

I decided to take a one-week intensive class on "Opening to Intuition." On the first night of the class, we sat around a fire outside, just getting to know each other and doing sacred ceremony in nature. I had difficulties due to my allergies. During the ceremony, I had my eyes closed for a minute trying to center myself. All of a sudden, I felt this amazing golden light surround my body, particularly my head. I was filled with the most peaceful, joyful, blissful feeling I had ever experienced. I heard a voice in my mind say: "I am Mother Mary and I am here to help you." After opening my eyes from the golden light experience, I stared at the amazing colors and patterns of the flames in the fire. I then saw Jesus, and he began to communicate telepathically with me, transmitting messages.

So I had to ask: Why would a Jewish girl from Skokie, Illinois, be seeing Jesus in the fire? And if all this happened on Day One, what would I experience during the rest of this class? The class was staying at a lake house containing many different energies and forces. To say it was haunted would be an understatement. Needless to say, I did not sleep very much that first night — or the nights that followed. I was simply overwhelmed.

The next morning, the class began a guided imagery activity. Suddenly, I saw swirling white lights, then prismatic lights, then I actually felt my third eye open and blink. There was no turning back after this: I was on the mystical path that I had tried to block. After the swirling and blinking stopped, I saw Atlantis, witnessed how the pyramids were built and viewed other ancient civilizations and technologies. I was flooded with information; it just kept downloading. I didn't know how to stop it. I saw the double helix, our DNA. I didn't know what it was at the time, because I had never seen it before — but I was able to explain DNA like I had studied it all my life. I saw genetic disorders and tools to discover them. I saw all types of healing arts. I asked so many questions that day and disrupted the entire class so often that the instructor banned me from asking any more questions until the last day of class. The more information I received, the more questions I had, and the more information I continued to get.

I felt fully alive and part of something greater than myself for the first time in my life. I was having this extreme metaphysical experience. I felt completely ungrounded in the presence of a teacher who wanted to see what else I could do. However, as I continued to raise my personal vibration, I also experienced a negative side effect: nosebleeds. I had three in a six-hour period. I was holding so much energy in my field without being aware of what to do with it or how to process it.

One evening during class, as we began to create mandalas as gifts for each other, I started to panic. An overwhelming fear came over me. For some reason, leaving the group did not seem like a viable option. Instead, I repeated over and over again, "I can't draw, you can't make me do this, and I refuse," interrupting the class for more than 45 minutes. I ended up doing the activity anyway. The class then began a guided journey to meet the guide of the person for whom each of us was creating an image. This went smoothly. When I looked down at the image I had created, it was unlike any other in the room. Mine was a precise image, designed for a specific purpose. It was drawn scientifically, down to the colors and patterns. The longer I looked at it, the more I realized that the mandala would help balance this individual's lazy eye. This experience turned out to be one of the greatest gifts I have ever received — and I have not stopped drawing since that fateful night.

Soon, the class ended and it was time to say goodbye to everyone and try to return to my regular life. I didn't live far from this teacher's center, and I learned that she was repeating the one-week intensive class over a 12-week period. She recommended it to help me integrate the experiences from the initial class, and I wanted that. But what was supposed to be 12 weeks turned into 16 more weeks of mystical experiences — while I was simultaneously breaking in at a new job I had just started. Had I not been a therapist with a background that included a week of mystical adventure, I probably would have been committed to my local hospital. How do you begin to tell the average person about such experiences, let alone therapists whose job it is to rule out psychosis? The adventure became even more interesting.

As the years have passed, more and more of my gifts have returned, and I am more comfortable talking about them and helping others. I have created more than 1,400 images, including mandalas that help people heal and balance, images for loved ones who have departed and babies coming into the world, logos and even a couple of tattoos. I do intuitive readings and healings, and I practice and use all of the different healing arts that I have studied.

I now look forward to what the next chapter has in store for me and how I will continue to share my gifts with humanity to awaken and move gracefully into the new energy of the earth and live from the heart. This is why Gail Alexander Energy Mandalas Facebook page *[www.facebook.com/GailAlexanderEnergyMandalas]* was created: To help others share the journey, connect through the heart and awaken to all that is — especially to our connection with each other.

 Gail Alexander is an Artist, Therapist and Energy Worker - Gail is a licensed professional counselor working in an Outpatient Eating Disorder Program. She also works as an intuitive and energy worker, incorporating the many healing arts she has studied. Gail draws upon these healing arts and her intuitive abilities to create energy infused mandalas. Each mandala is hand drawn and holds a specific frequency and vibration derived from the   principles of sacred geometry universal knowledge love, and light. When Gail draws, she allows the colors and shapes to flow through her as she creates each mandala and writes a channeled message.

https://www.facebook.com/GailAlexanderEnergyMandalas
http://www.gailalexandermandalas.com

Meet Mercedes Ortiz Baeza of *Calma Interior*

My name is Mercedes Ortiz Baeza and I am the creator and administrator of the Spanish Facebook page, "Calma interior." Welcome to a meeting with my story!

Looking back at a time when I was not fully aware, today I can see that I was getting ready for Calma interior to come into my life. Its birth was deeply desired! My soul longed for the creation of this page. Paths full of images, phrases, poems, writings and books, all of which caught my attention, guided me! Books and magazine articles aroused all kinds of emotions in me, and my world was transformed. Sometimes I had to write, and at other times read, but overall my mind was overflowing with inspiration. I sat at the computer and allowed my soul to create and express itself. I felt so much freedom during these moments, and I realized that this was the place that I wanted to be — and a place for others to come and nourish their souls.

Calma interior, thus, became my place, my refuge — a place where kindred spirits came to reunite. It is here where my mind is still, where it spreads its wings and can "be." It is the fusion between my mind and my heart, between my thoughts and emotions. You cannot describe what you feel when you discover and connect with your gifts and talents, when love and passion are your teachers and the magical world of creativity opens wide before you. Wonderful colors and doors continue to open, inviting me to explore the unknown, and not feel fear. I feel as though I am guided by a higher purpose that enlightens and sustains me.

I know that everything has to happen, as all things happen in due time....

After having traveled long roads, where life put me in front of people and situations helped me in my growth and evolution, now I can really thank life from the bottom of my heart for everything I have experienced, for all I have learned and am still learning.

At one point, life called me to wake up. All I had built until then began to crumble — breaking, breaking...dying slowly. Suddenly, everything I had in my life was just not there — relationships, family, work, structures — first life whispered in my ear, and then I could hear it shouting at me, screaming one very important word: change! It was easy to understand and learn the art of letting go, to live with detachment, closing stages that had already run their course. There were growing pains and there were years in which I lived with the dark night of my soul, when I cried myself to leave no tears, where sadness was my constant companion. But now, I realize I had to go through what I went through to be who I am today. It was, and still is, a long road of self-knowledge. The only way to begin to heal my wounds was through direct contact with the deepest pain — and I would go slowly, dying and being reborn, into a strengthened, better version of me. I learned to lose the fear of my vulnerability, dropping those protective walls that prevented me from being myself.

Something inside me told me I was growing up, that I was maturing.

"Crossing rivers and seas, I grew up to become the woman I am today...and freedom in the soul and love in my heart, my flight, now more than ever, pointing to the sky, my flight is all-encompassing. Today I laugh, there is joy in my life and I encourage you to be happy. "

This was a process in my life that demanded change, action and patience, all formidable skills.

All of this awakened a great need for connection, and it opened up my heart, ultimately leading me to create my Facebook page. Life teaches me so much every day. By giving without expecting to receive, I learned so much, but I receive back so much more than I ever could have imagined. Such nice people have identified with Calma interior and have joined my journey with love and respect, vibrating with a word, catching up and feeling that we are all one. This is what drives me to continue to share my inner world. Vibrating with the energy of love, sunlight, with the joy of living! Conceive of life as a great gift and the hug here and now with faith, trust, commitment and optimism.

This page is a balm for my soul and is the bridge that connects me to the world through love, compassion, inspiration, creativity, wisdom and joy.

I feel fulfilled doing what I like, what I receive effortlessly — what gives me pleasure. This I call "happiness."

Thanks to everyone who has crossed my path to guide me and teach me the only universal language that unites us all — that language of LOVE.

Mercedes Ortiz Baeza is a mother of three children who teach her every day to become a better person. She has studied Astrology and now works as a Floral Therapist. She is happy helping and inspiring others to live life to its greatest fullness. Her other passions are books, travel, contact with nature and, of course, her new Facebook page "Calma interior" at

https://www.facebook.com/pages/Calma-interior

Meet Anthony J. Diaz – Inspirational Empowerment Facilitator and Coach's Status

Heeding The Call: It's My Story and It's Sticking to Me . . .

I was born to live on this Earth;
To be myself, to know my worth.
I am free to be me, to live my truth.
I have my faith, no need for proof.

When you know you have all you need,
With water, soil - just plant the seed.
When you have all you need to know,
Nothing to do but let it grow

I wake each day living my dream,
Speaking my truth, no lack of esteem.
I am free to be me, the life I choose
Everything to gain, and nothing to lose.

The words danced off my pen on the page and I couldn't write them fast enough. My mind was swirling with feelings and thoughts as I flew home from California. I had been there before and was never quiet fond of it but this time...this time was different. For the first time, I travelled the 18 mile scenic highway from Pebble Beach which had always been a dream of mine. I saw the Pacific Ocean like never before...its power, its passion, its purpose. It was majestic yet quite humble in its own way. It sang its song of freedom, it spoke of wisdom, it called to me. This was not the first time I heard the call but now it was time.... time to heed the call.

The Taps

My whole life has been a calling in some form or fashion. Since my childhood as a young boy I have been following a path, I just didn't know it at the time. I had been raised for the most part by women - my mother, aunt and grandmother. This was one of the happiest times of my life. Their influence on me would set the stage for my evolving as a man and continuing through my spiritual consciousness and transformation. Growing up with my mother, I learned quite early the challenges she faced as a single parent, acting as the man of the house early on and being compassionate in times of others sadness and grief. I didn't quite understand it at the time but it seemed natural to be and act in this way. It seemed like only yesterday when I would hold my mother telling her it was OK when I felt like she needed it. I didn't know why but it felt like the right thing to do.

As I grew up, I begin to understand that my life was beat to a different drummer. I felt like I was not like others through high school and even in college. I never took the road most travelled instead choosing the path that seemed to open up choices for me. I gravitated toward forks in the road identifying with the song so eloquently written by Dan Fogelberg "Netherlands" where he spoke of such a fork in the road not knowing which way to go. He nailed it for me when he reaffirmed what I knew along that it didn't matter which one you took...It was all Good!

One such fork in the road occurred when I was working part time in a hospital kitchen and cafeteria while going to college as an Accounting major. A full time entry-level position had opened up in the Accounting department there and I applied for it. If I were hired, I would be working full time during the day and would have to transfer my studies to the evening.

My friends and family questioned my decision and wondered if I would ever be able to graduate if I undertook this position. I had the knowing...I felt the tap...I saw the fork in the road and I could see the possibilities. It wasn't that my family and friends did not have faith in me but they didn't and couldn't see what I saw...couldn't feel what I felt. I knew what that tap was and I acted upon it. During this time, I was reading Seize the Day by Saul Bellows in college.

This was perfectly synchronistic as I spoke of this book while being interviewed for this full time accounting position. When I was asked why I was seeking this job and would I be able to juggle the hours of work and school, I would quote from Saul Bellows and respond that this was a chance for me to seize the day. This was the fork in the road that I knew which one to take. I ultimately was hired for the position, which reaffirmed my belief and faith in listening to the tap.

The Nudges

Having listened to the taps many times in my life, it was clear that these were opportunities to pay attention, to heed the call. When you don't listen to the taps or don't even hear them, the Universe has a way of getting your attention in other ways. These ways are a little more noticeable just to make sure you don't miss them. Many times, I had been given taps during relationships...messages to guide me that I chose not to listen to. I heard them all right but I didn't trust them.

Usually, when we don't listen to the opportunities we are given its either that we need to learn the lesson from not heeding them or we don't trust ourselves to take action. Maybe we feel it will be too painful or the action we need to take is too unknown and we'd rather stay with what we know. Whatever the reason is, we are always given other chances in the form of a nudge. I had to learn many lessons in relationships so I usually ignored the taps. There was growth I had to experience and in that growth I understood what the nudge was all about. Although I didn't listen to the taps, I am so grateful to learn from these experiences, which helped to create the foundation of a strong committed intimate relationship that followed.

A nudge I did pay attention to after ignoring the initial taps before led me back to school to get my law degree after being out of school for twelve years. After listening to the tap that led me in getting my accounting degree while working full time in the accounting department, I went from job to job looking for what I couldn't find. Each time I found myself bored with what I was doing, I was being tapped to search within for what would be fulfilling. But instead I took the easy way out and found the next best position until the cycle repeated itself again. Not until these taps became nudges did I understand that until I busted loose from my current career would I give myself an opportunity to live the life I desired. Once I listened to the nudges, I realized that my dream of being a lawyer whom I dismissed early as a senior in high school could still be achieved. That twenty-year dream was realized once I graduated from law school at the age of 39.

The Two by Fours

Having experienced the taps in my life and knowing the feeling of getting the nudge, I have also ignored both ways of getting my attention. These have not happened very often, but when they did it felt like getting smacked in the back of the head with a two by four. Let me tell you, that definitely made me notice!

Two of the most significant of these happened before and after my mother was diagnosed with a terminal illness. Up until that point we always had a loving and challenging relationship. I was always the independent one testing boundaries and this way of being also tested our relationship. When she was given only months to live, the two by four came swiftly and with a force never before experienced.

Throughout the years, the taps and nudges were there as our mother and son dance would continue and fluctuate. When the news came of her illness, I was in Atlanta, GA visiting my aunt. I immediately flew home and began a four month exercise of getting her affairs in order, moving her to be with my aunt, winding down my life in Stamford, Ct and relocating myself to be near her side. That little boy kicked in and finished what he started with his mother years ago. In those last days and weeks, we were able to have the relationship I had been tapped and nudged so many times before.

Long before my mother was diagnosed, I had decided to take some time from my ongoing reconnecting with my father who was not a significant part of my growing up which I leave for another time. This time right before the two by four previously mentioned about my mother's illness struck, I decided to reach out and connect again with my father. Not even knowing why at the time, I told him that I wasn't sure why but it felt like the right time. Only later did I realize that listening to this call would lead to a reconnection with one parent that would serve me well through and after the transition of the other.

Although I now realize that my calling is to inspire and empower those who seek to have purpose and meaning in their life, I needed to experience the taps, nudges and two by fours in my own life to understand this journey. I had to experience my own inspiration and empowerment so that I could walk on the path with others to do the same. The last call I answered before I knew this was the life I was meant to live was while at a spiritual retreat in Pacific Grove, CA. Again, I was called by the ocean to fully understand my own magnificence —while embracing the powerful and purposeful passions that were ready to be realized and embodied and expressed. As I heeded the call, I now understand my story and why it's sticking to me.

As I watch the Pacific Ocean
My intention I envision
is continue my devotion
with certainty, love and decision

Like the waves crashing in the morn
I see my unlimited possibilities abound
my powerful, purposeful passions are born
to embrace new beginnings without a sound

This is the time to release and let go
and embody my abundant co-creation
I have all I need to be and grow
This is my magnificent manifestation

The time is now to be your magnificent manifestation so that you ca live a life of purpose and meaning.

I know this for myself, I know this for you and so it is. !n-Joy! Namaste.

Anthony J. Diaz has more than a decade of practicing family law and mediation, and is considered a leader in the area of collaborative law. As an attorney and a life and spiritual coach, Anthony incorporates a healthier approach to empower those going through a divorce or any legal or personal challenge by going within themselves and understand how their outer circumstances are affected by their inner conflict. Through personal and professional training and experience, Anthony has guided many who seek inspiration and empowerment to live a life of purpose and meaning NOW.

www.anthonyjdiaz.com
www.orlandomediationarbitration.com
www.facebook.com/IAmOnPurpose
www.twitter.com/#/IAmOnPurpose/ or @IAmOnPurpose
www.linkedin.com/in/orlandolitigateormitigate
www.blogtalkradio.com/collaborativelyspeaking/

Meet Suzie Nichols of *Always Leave em' Laughing*

IN EARLY CHILDHOOD, I experienced some difficult times that left me feeling vulnerable and had my self-esteem suffering a bit. I was bullied in grade school and began to use humor to deflect the blows. By middle school, I had learned to joke about anything that made me uncomfortable, and I began to see my life shift. Throughout high school and college, you would never have known that I struggled with self-esteem. I became active in sports, chorus, and student government. All of these activities served as outlets for me to toss out that well-placed joke, or even to make myself the joke. For example, in a high school chorus performance, during a dance number, my skirt fell down and I ran off of the stage screaming. The school audience erupted in laughter, so I repeated the same episode for the parents later that evening. In college, I often used my sense of humor to promote a cause for the student government, and I dressed up as a clown for children's or charity events.

In 1992, I met a man who seemed nice enough. We dated for about two years. It was a time when he was "down on his luck," so he moved in with me. Not long afterward, he began using alcohol and other drugs.

That's when the abuse began. Later, I would learn that he had been in and out of halfway houses for many years. When he would come home drunk, high or stoned, I would go through all of his things and flush the offending substance. Of course, this never solved the problem. He was a decent guy when he was sober, a scary man when under the influence!

At first, it doesn't seem like abuse. It starts off subtly and becomes much more tangible in time. At first, they call you fat and you think to yourself, "Maybe I have put on a few pounds lately." Once you've grown used to that, it escalates into things like "ugly" or "useless." Before you even realize what's happening, your self-esteem has become so eroded that you start to think you actually deserve the name-calling. In my case, it didn't take long for the emotional abuse to become physical. I endured a lot of that during those years. I often feared for my own life. I began to use humor to deflect some of the emotional and physical blows. For example, when he would call me "fat," I would refer to the fact that things expand when heated, saying, "I'm not fat, I'm just hot!" When others noticed the bruises, I would make some crack about my lack of coordination and would invent a story about walking into doors or tripping on curbs.

It was bad enough that I tolerated his abuse myself; when I became pregnant, I KNEW that my priorities needed to change. I had to put the welfare of my child first. During the pregnancy, that meant making some very difficult financial decisions, including letting my house be foreclosed upon, and moving to a rental property. This would at least ensure that I could provide for my child financially. The physical abuse continued throughout, and after, the pregnancy. The day came when I began to fear for the safety of my son. It was time for me to become strong. I needed to remove myself, and my beloved child from that situation.

Because this book is all about inspiration — and NOT victimization — I will simply say that, if not for my sense of humor, I don't know how I would have survived those years. I found the strength and the will to get out of that situation, not just for myself but for my son. I was not at all sad to see that one in the rearview mirror!

In 2000, I met a wonderful man. I saw all of the "stars, rainbows and sunshine" that come with a new relationship. We dated for four years before we married in 2004. You would think that I would have seen the signs in four years, but I didn't. I honestly did not see the abuse coming at all. The emotional abuse began almost immediately after we married. He was continuously putting me down and laughing when his blows would hit their mark. He would call me fat, ugly, and anything else that garnered a reaction from me.

Just three years into the marriage, it was clear this was not working at all. I begged him to go to counseling, and he refused, calling it "psychological crap." Because it was financially enabling, we shifted from living as husband and wife to living as roommates — sharing a house but not living quarters. We still shared pets and had to talk about expenses. Whenever I needed to have a conversation with him, he would refuse to speak to me in the moment, forcing me to "make an appointment!"

He was not working and was still expecting me to support him. When I finally stopped buying groceries and paying bills for him, he secretly filed for bankruptcy. In his filing, he included a truck that was listed in both of our names. I had been making the monthly payments for the previous five years and I loved that truck!

Of course, the time had come when we clearly should no longer be living under the same roof. I hesitated to make the break, because this man had been around for most of my son's young life. Even though he was not a "role model" by any stretch of the imagination, my husband was still an important part of my son's life. It was painful for him to hear his stepfather tell him that he would not be seeing him anymore. That's right: he told my SON that he was moving out before he told me! It was a full year after he moved out that our divorce was finally ready to move forward. He had refused to file, because he wanted to stay on MY health insurance. I was the one who finally had to file.

Essentially, I had felt like I had been a single parent from the moment my son was born. Neither his biological father nor his stepfather could be counted on to care for him, help him with homework or just do the kinds of things that men do. Instead, it's just been my son and me for all of these years.

After the divorce, it took me a while to feel comfortable in my own skin again. I needed to heal and was looking for inspiration. I discovered so many incredible Facebook pages offering motivational and inspirational content. I absolutely adored looking at all of them. Something was still missing for me, though. I both wanted and NEEDED to be able to laugh! I needed to laugh at my own pain — and laugh through all of my struggles. I needed to heal myself, and in the process, I wanted to help others heal, as well. I had always been told how funny I was, so people began to suggest that I start a page on Facebook. My self-esteem was beginning to bounce back, and I wondered if my friends and family were just building me up with compliments, or if it could really work. Eventually, I decided to find out.

I started "Always Leave em' Laughing" *[www.facebook.com/ Alwaysleaveemlaughing]* on January 8, 2012. For the first few weeks, I shared humorous content, despite the fact that nobody had actually "liked" my page. On January 23, I received my first "like." I stumbled upon some of the wonderful websites that allow you to download and edit photos, and I began playing with some photos of my own. One day, I used a photo of my beloved dog who had recently passed away. I added captions and "overlays," turning it into a funny photo.

Not long afterward, I noticed a Facebook page that had displayed that photo of mine with the name of my page cropped out. I wrote to the page owner in a very light and non-confrontational way. I explained that this photo was taken by me, edited by me, and used on my page. I said that I was not sure how it had ended up on her page without my name on it. Within 20 minutes, the page owner not only apologized to me, but she recommended my page to all of her followers. My Facebook page's reach jumped by about 300 "likes" over night, while I was sleeping! Since that time, "Always Leave em' Laughing" has taken on a life of its own. As this segment is being written, "Always Leave em' Laughing" has more than 21,000 fans!

I absolutely love it when I get messages from readers who thank me, saying they really needed to laugh. That's what it's all about for me. Sometimes life is hard. A LOT of times life is hard. When you can learn to laugh about things, the difficulty disappears. As I have healed, so has my son. His father has been in rehab and has been clean and sober for some time now. My son gets to see him weekly and their relationship has grown.

I have grown so much through the creation and maintenance of this page! It has helped me heal my own heart, and it has brought joy and healing to others. I have had the pleasure to meet and interact with a number of other Facebook page administrators whom I am now proud to call "friends." Often, people think that you're selfless for creating a Facebook page for the benefit of others. I don't feel selfless, and it's not JUST for the benefit of others. I get every bit as much out of running my page as I give! Nothing makes me happier than to "Always Leave em' Laughing."

Suzie Nichols is $39.95 plus shipping & handling; at least that's what she tells people who ask her age. She lives in Northern Virginia and has worked with adults with special needs for 24 years. She can't imagine doing anything else. She also loves to sing, attend outdoor concerts, and make people laugh. She grew up with two brothers and a sister who now have children of their own. Her parents live in Tennessee. She has one INCREDIBLE son who is almost 16, and a miniature Dachshund named Oscar Mayer. Oscar is a favorite on "Always Leave em' Laughing." Visit

https://www.facebook.com/Alwaysleaveemlaughing

Meet Lori Rubenstein of *Freedom From Abuse - Finding Yourself Again with Coach Lori Rubenstein*

Courageous Journeys

I KNEW MY COLLEGE-AGED children were on line and involved in something called "Facebook." It was a place for kids to hang out and, I believed, flirt with each other. I figured it was something like the social networking site, Myspace, and that the kids would eventually grow out of it.

In 2008, I went to my 30th high school reunion. Everyone started saying, "let's keep in touch," "let's all get on Facebook!" Un-tech-savvy me had to figure out how to do this, which I did. Naïve me thought my kids would be happy I was being so hip! I quickly learned that my son would not "friend" me. So naturally I worried about what was on HIS page. (Yes, of course I found ways to look!) When my daughter did "friend" me, I was out of my mind seeing all the partying she was doing. I quickly learned that Facebook was a way to "spy" on my kids and drive myself crazy with TMI (too much information!) LOL!

Shortly after entering the world of Facebook, I read a very funny article written by a mother whose children would not "friend" her. I started connecting with other mothers. It turned out that mothers my age were the largest growing group on Facebook! However, when my own mother (I honestly have NO idea how she managed to get on!) suddenly "friended" me, I was devastated. I didn't want her to know what I was doing! Inter-generationally, we were all spying on one-another and, simultaneously, we all complained about each other to both friends and family! I was constantly getting in trouble for what my daughter was doing! It was too much!

Tired of spying on my children, I learned that I could also start connecting with friends and clients. Marketing experts said I should use Facebook as a marketing tool, but I soon discovered I really didn't like the marketing gig. I just liked the connections. I have made friendships with people all over the world! Everywhere I go, I am sure there is a Facebook buddy I can connect with! What a blessing that is! So, I stopped marketing and started connecting.

There is a big gift in using this social networking site, learning from each other & sharing our lives. Asking people to pray when a friend's child is hospitalized and realizing that hundreds of prayers, love and light are directed towards that person! People wanting help to get out of abusive situations have ways out they never had before! People dealing with the death of loved ones, divorce, losing homes and inspirational stories of overcoming hardships are all shared on the pages of Facebook. It's a treasure trove of what the world is like in the early decades of the 2000s. I wonder, if these pages were found 500 years in the future, what would those people think about our struggles, loves and passions?

Another blessing of connecting with all these people is to instantly have friends there with you, celebrating your successes. A new book, a new car, a marriage at almost 50 years old, weight loss, and climbing your first mountain! When I turned 50, I had close to 200 people take a minute of their time to say happy birthday. Honestly, the days leading up to 50 were difficult for me, and those messages, first thing in the morning just put me over the edge. From worrying about age to being excited and realizing that I'm in better shape at 50 than I was at 30! Gratitude set in and worries left.

I have decided, at least for now, to keep all my contacts, business, clients, friends, and acquaintances on one page, my personal page. I am like an open book anyway. My clients know I am human and since I adore the idea of VULNERABILITY, I allow them to see my own vulnerabilities. TOGETHER, we face life head on, with courage and the support of loving friends.

As a divorce attorney turned mediator turned divorce coach turned forgiveness teacher, I am able to relate to many people going through difficult transitions. I like to think of these as Courageous Journeys, as these are the times we really learn what we are made of. On Facebook, we are able to all support each other in those journeys. We share inspirational quotes and pictures and connect by telling our own stories. We relate to each other by sharing our tales of how we were able to make it through our tough times - our dark night of the soul moments.

For me, laughter is imperative. It's important to lighten things up and be able to laugh at oneself. I believe this is one of my greatest gifts. I'm all about "this too shall pass" and people who work with me, know it. We are able to laugh as well as cry together, and in this way, we can get through anything.

You can get a good flavor of my page with these most recent examples of postings on my page: In less than 2 weeks, people saw me come back from a glorious trip to Victoria, B.C. and post a video I took of a mother raccoon saving her babies from drowning, to discovering my son was in an accident with my car. My Facebook friends reminded me what a blessing it was that my son was OK even though my car was totaled. Good reminder, huh? A few days later, they got to see my new "hottie "red car and just a few days after that, my post about my new speeding ticket to go with my new "hottie" red car! The ups and downs of life are out there for everyone to see, and together, we can laugh and cry, pray and celebrate, dance and yes, even crawl when needed.

When you do not think you can make a difference in someone's life, think again.

In the middle of writing this, I checked in on my page and found someone thanking me for the 'heart lessons' of a video I shared. When Lori Rekowski asked me to write for this book, I told her, "No! I am NOT a big inspirational Facebook person!"

Fortunately, like any good coach, she yelled at me and forced me to look at the reality of the situation. So I did. I looked back at my page, and here are some examples of what I found. In response to my video on forgiveness: "I cried. I was pretty confident I had forgiven others. I realize now that the main person I haven't forgiven is myself. Thank you Lori, you inspire me," "Thank you, I really needed this today" and "Thank you for reposting, my daughter found it powerful." In response to a flower picture I took and added the words, "...Be at one with all that is and hear the loving thoughts of your soul," people told me I should make posters, write a book, and this one: "never thought of putting in the word 'loving' before soul, dah, good aha moment!"

We've had very intense, extended conversations about whether you can find your soul mate while you are married to someone else, to whether married couples should sleep in separate bedrooms. We've had lengthy discussions on how to protect yourself legally if you are not married but living together. We talk about thermography vs. mammography, as well as weight issues.

This community on my wall shares their vision boards, flowers blooming, meaningful songs and special times with friends and family. Everything in the last four years of my life is there, from living in Costa Rica, break-ups, getting remarried, happy times with Feminine Ground Retreat participants, and Soul Regression Therapy insights, to vacations and our amazing trip to Macchu Picchu, all shared with Facebook friends instantaneously.

We will continue to celebrate our triumphs and, together, support each other in working through grief. Life is all about these Courageous Journeys of ours. It is with honor that I participate in yours.

—Lori Rubenstein

 Lori S. Rubenstein, JD, CPC will tell you it is easy to be passionate about forgiveness when you see the healing power it has in so many lives. This divorce attorney turned relationship coach, author, and teacher, is a walking example of what can happen once you make the choice to be anything you want to be. She teaches, "Change is courageous, and not for sissies!" Whether you meet Lori in a workshop or through one of her transformational books, you are sure to be inspired by her mission of helping people break down their walls and heal the pain caused by broken relationships.

https://www.facebook.com/lorirubenstein
http://www.lorirubenstein.com/.
www.sedonasoulretreats.com
www.transcendingdivorce.com
http://www.loveadvicecoach.com
http://www.transcendingdivorce.com
http://www.sedonasoulretreats.com
http://heartjourneys.wordpress.com
http://www.sedonatalkradio.com
@lorirubenstein (Twitter)
relationshipcoach (Skype)

Meet Khuram Shahnawaz of
Golden Words of Paradise

MY NAME IS KHURAM Shahnawaz. I belong to Pakistan and currently I reside in Rawalpindi. By profession, I am an Anthropologist and have been working in Development sector since 2008. Being Anthropologist I always observe and behold things precisely and deeply, for me the most important is to find out the reasoning and logic behind everything. That is why being social scientist I love to interact with people of different cultures and societies. This interaction gives me enough sense to understand cultures and societies of others regions. I had been seeking after the opportunity to meet with new people of other regions and cultures since I joined Face book. The desire and aspiration to meet with new people brought me to social network site.

I joined Face book in 2011. At first, I was considerably fascinated by it for me it was a new world and horizon, which was imbued with surprises, excitement and energy. I had enough chance to meet with new people and discover the other worlds. I was going to be carried away by the spell of Face book. After a while all the excitement, ardor and enthusiasm began to die down. I could not figure out why I lost my interest and excitement in it. I felt one thing desperately that Face book lacked in the exchange of ideas and proper communication. People usually use it for their personal interest and fun and it is turning into dating site.

We all log in on Face book from various regions and countries and we need to know one another cultures, society, religion, cultural events, social traditions, cultural norms values and the most important their thoughts. What do they think about the universe? What is their opinion of world politics? How do they analyze the problems and issues of the world? What are their ideas to make this world a better place to live there? All these questions kept pinching me and lingered on in my mind for a long time and I was very keen and anxious to get to know the answers of them.

In the present time, the concept of SOCIAL INTERACTION has changed with advent of concept of Global Village. We all believe that this World has transformed into Global Village. This concept brings us closer to one another. Social Network sites give us enormous chances to interact with one another.

Nowadays our world is afflicted with abundance of problems. We all are grappling with many issues. These issues beget from our social life. We all have common problems namely poverty, inflation, illiteracy, crime ignorance, economic crisis and political instability. If we recall in the revolution of Egypt in our minds that ensued last year then we get to know it took place due to social network when some persons protested against the gruesome and outrageous policies of dictatorship and that protest turned into the greatest revolution. All the change came in Egypt through Face book. In present age no one can negates the worth and significance of social network sites. A great number of people are connected through it and this ratio is going up rapidly.

I must say that social network sites cast a deep and profound spell over the hearts of millions of people. They are very effective and dynamic sources to interact with new people and express our views about various issues. These sites give us enough liberty to reveal our opinion. I want to use them as a tool or weapon that stir up people to get closer and together.

I was very impressed with some pages, which are very inspirational and motivational. Then an idea to create a page struck in my mind so I decided to create a page on Face book named *Golden Words of Paradise*. The basic concern to create this page was to bring the people of other countries closer and generate awareness, harmony, and solidarity amongst them. I intended to form a page where people could express their opinion, thoughts and exchange their ideas with other people and Golden Words of Paradise provides them with bountiful chances to express themselves in very distinctive and unique manner. I motivate other people to express what they have in their mind right now. All my quotes are about life and love. I aim at disseminating love, harmony, light of spirit and soul, solidarity and universal peace through my page, I am quite lucky to be surrounded by such great and intellectual people who encourage me much to share and post more, and more stuff on page.

I am very grateful to my dearest friend Kathy and Karen for believing in me as well as in my ability and motivate me to share my story with them. Last but not the least Golden words of paradise just a beginning and I will keep moving on until I get to my destination. My destination is to make this world a better and prosperous place where all live happily in peace and they are treated equally beyond color, race, creed, and cast, ethnic and territorial identity. It is possible if we join our hands together for it.

Name: Khuram Shahnawaz
Country of origin: Pakistan
City: Rawalpindi
Occupation: Anthropologist
D.O.B: 30-06-1978
Hobbies: Reading, writing, net surfing and sports
Qualification: Mac in Anthropology
Page: *Golden Words of Paradise*
https://www.facebook.com/pages/Golden-words-of-Paradise/219719701429064

Meet Henriette Eiby Christensen of *110 Ways*

I was 30 years old in 1992 when I first read Robin Norwood's "Women Who Love too Much" and felt like I understood everything that had happened to me in my relationships and why. It was like falling in love with life.

I went to a support group, but didn't stay long. I felt the others were much worse off than I. Besides, I had a new boyfriend who seemed absolutely perfect - understanding and accepting me, bringing me flowers and gifts, writing me tons of letters... So I quit. I got pregnant within the first month of our relationship. In fact we did everything the opposite way than others normally do. First I got pregnant, then he moved in, and then we went out on a date. Needless to say, I was instantly stuck – dragging my three year old into what turned out to be a verbally abusive relationship.

In 2006, 12 years and two more children later, I came out of that relationship not knowing what had happened. Hurt, confused, depressed, and so full of regrets – the latter mostly because of what I'd put my eldest son through.

My ex-husband is a very handsome and smart man. I had always been more passive, a pleaser. I was willing to move and turn every single ounce of my body and soul to accommodate his needs. Why I believe I took the abuse so freely was because that there was an element of truth to every abusive thing he said about others or me, so I was kept in a state of constant confusion and soul searching. He never hit me. He never came home drunk. But he killed me a thousand times with his mouth. This man was my husband. We shared a bank account.

I did everything wrong– the way I kept our house wasn't how he liked it. I had too much "stuff." I was too "laid-back." He used "positive" critique to belittle me. He would cover his verbal abuse up in "I'm only being honest." He would call me names, and so many more horrific things I care not recall. My friends and family slowly evaporated from my life.

Here is the part, which is very hard to explain... why I stayed. I understand that this is sometimes difficult to comprehend from an outsider looking in. You see, I was a stay-at-home mom in Denmark and very isolated. In Denmark, being a stay-at-home mom is frowned upon. Having a job is much more valued. So I was alone - alone in my beliefs that my children were much more important than any job could possibly be. I felt that I didn't have children to have other people take care of them. I wanted to be the one to raise them.

An easy target you might say. Yes. I no longer had a network. I no longer had an income. I had no self-esteem or self-worth. No special skills, which might help me, create an income. My education was outdated. And I was stuck - emotionally and financially.

One day, he decided that we needed a second income, so he pushed me to work. I promptly got a job as a substitute teacher while my youngest was in kindergarten. A couple of years later, I went back to school to get a teaching degree (his idea). Well, guess what? I started socializing. I discovered I was smart. My classmates would call me for help with homework, and they valued my opinion. As I said – working was his idea, and it was he who pushed me into getting a degree so I could earn more money for our family. But every time I had an exam, he would threaten me with divorce, belittle me, and say phrases like: "You're really going to let your studying come before the well-being of this family and our children?" Well, the more of those he came up with, the harder I studied, and along the way my education became my life raft. It represented financial freedom and social connection. And – most importantly – it represented being valued for who I am as a human being. It saved my life.

I was relieved when he left, and I quietly celebrated with my now 14-year-old son who could not believe it had finally happened. In the ensuing months, I couldn't understand why I felt so bad, and kept feeling like the world would be a better place without me in it. I would still appreciate that he wasn't there, but I just didn't get why I was so tired and upset all the time. I could barely get the kids up in the morning, fix their lunches and make dinner – I just wanted to stay in bed and kill myself.

One day, depressed, I sat alone at my kitchen table – the kids in school. I got mad, so very angry. No way was I going to let him continue to have that kind of power over me. I had to understand everything, and so I started observing and writing. In the writing process, I had various women read my stuff, and it turned out this wasn't just my own private venture - it hit home with so many others it wasn't funny. It was actually scary how many could relate to my words. I wasn't alone. Comments like: "Oh my, you have written my story" began arriving in my email. I released it as a book, and started a Facebook support group.

I continued writing, and, five books later – all on bullying in relationships in Danish - I have amassed quite a following on my Danish site and groups.

In early 2012 I released my first book in English, *110 Ways to Detect a Bad Relationship,* and it hit the Amazon Hot New Releases list, as well as being mentioned in Forbes Women.

I hope to reach teens and young adults before they enter into long-term relationships before getting stuck, along with those who are in a "not-so-good relationship," who hopefully benefit from taking it home.

It is my wish to reach the educational systems all over the world with my book.

I also want to reach people who are stuck in bad relationships by helping them find out why they aren't happy, and giving them the courage to stand up for themselves.

I have come far, and writing helped immensely. So did talking, reading, and therapy. I have never been happier, which is why I believe I have reached a point when I can help and share. It just keeps getting better and better.

This has now become my life's purpose. I am a link between verbal abuse and happiness.

How can you avoid it?

By noticing how you feel, and appreciating your own self-worth. Always listen to your gut feeling – though that can be very hard, and very scary. But, practice makes perfect.

Here are just five of the biggest telltale signs in no particular order:

1. You are nervous around him (walking on eggshells.)

2. His needs come first (you drop everything at his call.)

3. Your friends and family disappear (they aren't good enough for you – he says.)

4. You suffer from various stress and anxiety symptoms (nausea, headaches, insomnia, dizziness, depression etc.)

5. You complain to yourself, or other people about him.

On a scale from 1 – 100 – how happy are you? Can you live with that? If a relationship isn't good – why be in it?

I have to emphasize here that not all men are bad, and while I write "he" and "him" roles are often reversed. I do it for the sake of simplicity, and because – obviously – I write from a woman's perspective.

I'm currently working on my next book, *110 Ways to Charm your Brain – Positive Thinking - Jewels collected since The Secret*. Hundreds of exercises, quotes, and questions to keep you on track, plus my own road to happiness and purpose.

 Henriette Eiby Christensen, Danish, born 1962, mother of three, Speaker, Counselor and Author of *110 Ways to Detect a Bad Relationship* and other books. You can find them at:

http://www.110ways.com
https://www.facebook.com/eibychristensen

Meet Marie Suk of *Body-Mind-Spirit-Integration and Healing*

My journey has been about moving from wounded warrior to goddess, and in the process, learning to own my victim. When I finally began to bring the victim in me out of my deepest darkest shadows and bathe it in acknowledgement, acceptance and unconditional love, I reached a new height of self-healing. This sweet surrender brought me closer to my divine feminine energies and allowed my battle-scarred and weary warrior to finally rest. I have learned that for me, the pushing, fighting and struggling only blocked the movement and flow of what was to be.

The more I became present in the moment, and turned my eyes inward towards myself and began to shine the healing light of unconditional love into my dark places, the more life unfolded for me in the most beautiful ways. I slowed down and allowed life and love to surround me, instead of rapidly running through each day to get to the next one. I am truly blessed to be living my authentic life, while I continue on my path of healing myself as I am helping others. I have only recently began to understand the message being whispered in my ear, "Make space and they will come." I needed to let go of what no longer served me to make room for the light. I have never actively sought out being a light worker. I just opened to my truth and followed my heart.

My story began more than 40 years ago. While I was still in the womb, my father abandoned me, deciding he did not want a wife or a child. My mother tried to reconcile with him, traveling from Korea to the States hoping he would have a change of heart. Unfortunately, a happy reunion is not part of this story.

Soon after I was born, my father and my grandparents conspired behind my mother's back to have a local woman adopt me and convince my mother to return to Korea to relieve my father of child support obligations. My mother could not be made to leave me; instead, she was wrongly committed to a psychiatric hospital and I was placed into foster care. It was only through the kindness of strangers that my mother was able to leave the hospital, find a job as a housekeeper and bring me home.

Deeply scarred, mentally and emotionally, my mother turned her anger towards the only one available, me. My childhood was a war zone full of physical, mental and emotional abuse, and as a result, I was taught some major dysfunctional lessons: emotional dishonesty, emotional suppression and to never fully trust anyone, especially men. She conditioned me to not only be her rescuer, but to be a warrior, dependent on no one, fearless, and feeling-less, everything she wanted to be.

The feelings of frustration and anger were overpowering, and so were thoughts of suicide. I felt as if nobody loved or wanted me. My life seemed meaningless. Some children are afraid of the dark and the monsters hiding within it. I hoped that the monsters would come and gobble me up. When I was about 12 years old, I specifically remember praying to God to give my life to a dying child who had loving and caring parents. I thought, "Why should I continue to live, as unloved as I am? What is the point?"

One thought kept popping into my head throughout my adolescence: I was being damaged in some unseen way and someday I would have to heal myself.

I left home when I was 16 after a particularly violent knock-down, drag-out fight. I continued to go to school while bouncing from place to place, feeling more alone, more unwanted, more out of control, and more angry.

In relationships, I was a man-eater — cruel and abusive — and I could go into a full-blown rage at any time, for any reason. I was completely numb and empty, never letting anyone into my heart. I had what I perceived to be total freedom for the first time in my life. Nobody was hovering over me, waiting for the opportunity to judge me, manipulate or hurt me. The way I fed my power and stayed in control was by alternately rescuing and victimizing others. It was all about my ego and me. Empathy was a word I just could not understand.

When I was 21, I experienced a powerful turning point. I looked into the mirror one day and I did not like what I saw. I did not like the road I was traveling and the emptiness I was feeling. I did not like me. I decided at that moment to change things. I abruptly disassociated with my core group of friends, broke up with my boyfriend, moved, joined a church and began therapy.

I loved therapy. I looked forward to going each week — and each week I moved mountains. My therapist recommended a few spiritual books on self-healing and I consumed them. One session in particular stands out. It was the session in which we were talking about the abuse I had suffered. She looked at me and simply said, "It was not your fault." She said it so casually, and it hit me so hard, that I physically winced as if I had been slapped in the face. My reaction took us both by surprise. She repeated what she had said once more, and I had the same reaction, but this time with a flow of tears that seemed endless. That message was the inspiration I needed to fully embrace my recovery.

At 23, I was making slow, but steady, progress in my self-healing, so I decided to take a giant step and reconnect with my grandmother. It ended up being a reunion with my father, who was a stranger to me. My mother had destroyed all evidence of him; consequently, I grew up not knowing what he even looked like.

I do not know exactly how to explain what happened to me, but the moment he walked into the room, my scarred, broken and guarded heart instantly opened, and I loved him. I never expected that. It took me by complete and utter surprise. I loved everything about him. I loved his wild hair and his beard. I loved his eyes, his hobbies and his career. If he had been a drunken, homeless person lying in the gutter, I would have loved that, too. I just overwhelmingly loved this man at first sight.

I didn't know most of the story I have told you about my mother's first few months in the United States until much later in my life. I only uncovered the facts around her hospitalization, because it became an issue for her after she applied for citizenship when I was 12 years old. The rest of the story — and more of the horrific details, most of which I have spared you — came from my grandmother, in a matter-of-fact way, as if she were dictating a grocery list — no emotion, no regrets, no apologies.

Contact with my father and my grandmother eventually waned. I could not continue my painful visits to my grandmother's house, and he never initiated any contact. He was always friendly and talkative when I called, but never interested in meeting. I felt as if I were chasing a ghost, so I stopped calling him.

Even though our contact virtually stopped, the abandonment, rejection and feelings of not being good enough continued to haunt me through many relationships. I attracted men into my life who reinforced these feelings.

In 1999, I experienced a life-altering event. I was still living in my ego-based reality. I had money, two vehicles, a beautiful apartment, expensive clothing and gorgeous jewelry. I worked long hours, even on the weekends, because I felt the need to overachieve in order to feel important. I turned down invitations to family functions, dinner with friends; I lived for my job, 24/7.

I have been psychic my entire life, inheriting gifts from both sides of my family, and now I began to receive warning signs: something big was coming. I would hear a boom and see a large, orange flash in my peripheral vision. The flash was so genuine that I would cry out, thinking it was fire.

One morning, on my way to work, I had a terrible car accident. It was severe and disfiguring, and it was my life's biggest blessing. It was a wake-up call to all that really mattered in life. It was not about my possessions. It was not my job or the money. It was not even about my physical body. It was much bigger. I began to realize that life was about love, and I received confirmation of that the night after I returned home from the hospital. I blissfully dreamed of God and was given a message.

From that day forward, I continued on a much deeper path of healing. I was guided to many extraordinary healers and mentors, each adding their own unique light to my journey. I still struggled, made mistakes and sometimes lost my way, but I never quit.

I would like to share with you the most powerful and personal healing event that happened to me. I was never able to get over the heartbreak of not being loved by my father. It was something that haunted me most of my adult life. One night, it became too much. I cried and cried, and through my tears I asked, "What is the gift in this?" My mind grew quiet, I went down deep into my heart and my father appeared — not the man who rejected me, but his true self, the one of pure light. I asked him, "Please tell me, what the gift in all of this is?" And he replied, "The gift in your rejection and abandonment is unconditional love." Through all the pain, all the sadness and all the hurt that he had caused, I was still able love him. He explained that I was created in light and love, and that all my life I had been waiting for him to rescue me, but what I was really waiting for was for me to rescue myself.

I was at peace. I knew my father's true essence was always with me in my heart, and I felt loved.

It is my sincerest intention for you, dear reader, that in unveiling some of my hidden wounds, my grief and my shame, you will know that you are not alone and true healing is within reach. The treasure I have found by sifting through the ashes of "victim" is my story. It is possible for you to find your bliss and to live your authentic life, even if you are currently stuck in darkness. The road to healing is one you must ultimately travel alone (only you know your truth), but your heart, your guides, the universe and those amazing angels disguised as humans are supporting and loving you throughout your journey. This I know to be true, and I am honored to share the message from the Creator: "What we take with us when we transition out of this life is all the love we have been given and all the love we have shared."

 Marie Suk is a Psychic, Professional Holistic Life Coach, Vibrational Sound Healing Practitioner, Certified Personal Trainer and Intuitive Healer located on Long Island in Rocky Point, New York. She also travels to Lancaster, Pennsylvania, to conduct private sessions and workshops. After a severe and disfiguring car accident in 1999, she awoke with a special message of LOVE from the Creator that serves as her guide. She performs all of her services with sincerest compassion, through the heart-center, setting the intention for your highest truth, light, wisdom, love and healing.

www.facebook.com/pages/Marie-Suk-Body-Mind-Spirit-Integration-and-Healing/219111134780931

http://www.iamhealingthrufeeling.com

Meet Marin Peterson of *Free Will Magnified*

I WANT TO TAKE A MOMENT and share with you the events of a personal story.

On November 22, 2002, my siblings and I were preparing for an exciting day. My parents, who had raised eight children, were moving into brand new surroundings after living on hand-me-downs and buying in bulk to meet the needs of a large family. My mother, the matriarch, kept order and sanity; my father, a good provider, maintained a quiet, safe place. Both would instill in us the importance of loving each other and being conscious of the less fortunate around us.

So it was moving day — a time for my parents to fulfill dreams and give to themselves what they had sacrificed for their children. They were so entitled, and we were all on board to contribute to a new chapter in their lives. The truck filled with "new" furniture was arriving at 9:30. Dad was sweeping the garage, Mom making coffee, awaiting the arrival of their children.

As I prepared to leave my house, I received a call that my mother found my father lying on the ground unconscious. I was distraught. I could barely take a breath. I couldn't think, couldn't drive, but somehow I arrived at the hospital. As I entered the waiting room, I found eighteen family members waiting. I remember scanning the crowd, looking for my mother. As a path clears, I found her broken and bewildered, and I took her into my arms. In my heart and in my head, I kept thinking, "God makes possible the impossible."

Complete organ shutdown was now taking place. I truly felt it necessary that we put God in charge. The crisis was far too great for eighteen people to carry. Only the hand of God could shift this awful event. Within two hours, life would begin to run through my father's veins. Over the next few days, the machines used to assist his kidneys, heart and breathing were no longer needed. Although my father remained in a coma, oxygen and food were the only necessities. And our Angel slept.

Our lives shattered. I can only speak for myself, but the absence of my father consumed me. He was my first love. I would compare every man to his greatness. Of course, that seemed unfair, but I knew I would always desire his beauty and attributes, and my life would always thirst for the remnants he left behind. The shift for me came when a small voice spoke out in my darkness. It was my daughter, who was 10 at the time. She said "God wouldn't put us here without a plan." BOOM! The light went on. My senses stirred. She was right! God speaks to us through the actions and words of others. He was here, in my space. Wherever I am, God is.

God has taught me over and over again that it's never the obvious — look to the left or to the right to see what it is really about. When events take place, they do so to shift other things in a positive way. I would now have to choose where I stand: in the darkness of my sleeping angel, or in the light of greater things. I could never cover my father's entire process, but I will show you how the hand of God was clearly present in our journey.

My father was transferred to a nursing home for further care, to avoid disconnecting his feeding tube and oxygen. [Personally, I am a firm believer that we should pass from this world as gracefully as we enter it. That call belongs to no one other than God — in this case, the agreement between my father and his maker.] After three weeks of hospitalization, my father was transferred. As the hospital prepared him to leave for the nursing home, my oldest sister visited him. My ex-husband arrived, as well, not knowing that my father was being moved. [Let me show you now just how precise God is.]

The nurse asked my ex-husband if he would like a map to my father's new residence. He indicated that he would like a map, and the nurse walked away, and then she returned with a map. After receiving it, my ex-husband looked up and said, "Aren't you my step-sister?"

Yes, indeed, it was his sister. Someone he hadn't seen in 25 years now stood before him. I will say it again: Events take place in order to shift other things. If my father is not in a coma, a brother does not find his sister. I will remind you often, just as God reminds me: It isn't the obvious: look to the left or the right to see what it is really about.

Family members gathered at the nursing home and awaited the paramedics. As they wheeled my father into his room, our group was quiet as the staff prepared him for bed, hooked up his IVs and settled him in for the night. We allowed the nurses and paramedics to tend to their procedures, and like a quiet thunder, the Holy Spirit let His presence be known. This would be the first of many visits.

In the midst of a flurry of activity, we heard a shuffling of feet. We all turned around to find the first sign of our "Angel." She was walking slowly. We came to know her as "Joanie." She was a 60-year-old Down syndrome patient, whom I'm sure was called here by God. She had only been here a few minutes, and we were perplexed as to why no one ushered her out. Slowly, she approached my father; we cleared out of the way and let her through — past the family, past the nurses, past the paramedics to my father, resting in his bed.

Her speech was a bit broken as she mumbled to my father, stroking his head. She looked up at all of us and said, "I am the nurse; he is the patient. I hear him and he hears me." [God speaks to us through the words and actions of others. He is behind every set of eyes — we saw Him and He spoke.] She would come to visit him multiple times throughout his days — talking to him and touching him just like angels do. Our large family had no problem taking her into our lives. Even in my father's waking life, he would have loved her as she loved him. We would give her no less.

I remembered some visits from God, and there were many that I did not; over the course of time here, they became too numerous to count. I recalled asking two nurses their names, as I always wanted to greet each of them personally. One was named Redemptia and the other Fatima. Think I missed it? Not for a second. I personally had many conversations with doctors regarding my father's right to receive food and oxygen. Too often, I felt at battle hanging onto the Declaration of Faith, which prohibited anyone from deciding the termination of the life of another. I reminded the doctors that this was not their call; it was God's. Then, the family — and especially my mother — was told that the doctors wanted to meet with us. I arrived shortly before the meeting, went into my father's room and got down on my knees and asked God to serve as intercession. I would have to accept whatever God had decided. I thank Him in advance, stood up and the nurse came in to inform me that the meeting had to be canceled. There was an emergency, and the doctors were called out. God makes possible, the impossible. Thank you God for one more day.

Every day, I wondered where I would see God again. During the next weeks and months, my father taught us how to communicate, even while he slept. And then, due to unforeseen circumstances, he was transferred to another nursing home. The home that God picked was "Shalom," meaning, "to be complete, perfect and full." Once again, He delivered and we were blessed. The nurse who came to care for my father was as beautiful as any angel could be. She was a beautiful black woman, whose family was back in Africa. She offered exceptional care, a warm blanket that would give our family a sense of peace and calm that we needed so desperately. One day I came to visit and found my father's door closed.

As I slowly entered, I heard Hawaiian music playing, representing one of my father's favorite places to visit. I walked into the room and found our Angel peacefully applying lotion to my father's feet and hands. Each day, my father took on more youthfulness as she pampered and extended her goodness. She cared for him so lovingly, and it was evident that he was as much a part of her as she a part of him. Thank you God for her presence.

She would later share that even while my father slept, he was giving of himself. On one occasion, my father's nurse was working on a different floor, and one of her patients was having breathing difficulties. She told me that caring for my father taught her skills that allowed her to extend the breath of life to someone else, because she knew to clear the airway. We were on the same page. We were allowing God to lead us, but in return, we would have to give it up to Him. I extended my sincere gratitude for all that our father's nurse, willingly gave to us. She told me that her own father was dying in Africa. She could not be there to care for him, therefore, she chose to pour her heart and soul into the life of my own father. And she did.

My father passed away in 2004. Choosing to be present in his journey was far safer than being suspended in the grief. I called my father's nurse to let her know that he had passed. When she entered the church the day of his funeral, we rushed to her once again. We needed to be lost in the comfort of her arms, feeling as though only she could heal our broken emptiness.

The final goodbye in the form of a miracle was yet to come. About two months later, I received a call from my father's nurse, and she told me that her father has passed. She could not afford to go home, as travel would involve passing through four countries to get to him. I wanted to embrace her pain as she did for me — and pull her close and return the warmth. I hung up the phone, and then I contacted my family and told everyone the news that she could not afford the cost of going home. We all disconnected for literally five minutes — then, my phone begins to ring. My mother told me that my father had many frequent flyer miles built up and we would give them to his nurse — and a kind contributor would come up with the rest —that, and then some. The kind contributor also made the arrangements and all the connecting flights to get my Dad's nurse home to Africa to bid farewell to her own beautiful father. In his own way, my father was able to say "thank you" for all of her undying love.

God will give definition to your life and its experiences. In doing what God asked me to do, it was about a brother finding a sister. It was about Joanie, the Down syndrome patient who assured us of her connection and God's message, and her need to be part of a loving family. It was about Redemptia and Fatima. It was also about extending the breath of life to another, and making it possible for a beautiful caregiver to go home to Africa to say her own goodbyes.

My father's life, even after his passing, was created with great purpose and meaning. If the event of his coma had not taken place, the string of blessings would never have occurred. My Dad gave beyond his final breath. God used my sleeping father as a vehicle to move others to higher ground. God took this solitary life and allowed it to bless the lives of many. My father became an instrument of God's peace. Let this be proof that all the good that my father's nurse willingly extended was withdrawn from her bank of graces and allowed to pour forth upon her to get her home again.

There is no greater Love on Earth than that of a loving God.

 Marin Peterson has participated in and promoted the Sri Chinmoy's Peace Concert, The Hastings Women's Expo, Mind, Body, Spirit Expo and the Wholeness Festival at the College of St. Catherine's in St. Paul, Minnesota. In her mission to showcase the gifts and talents in her senior community, she created the "Spotlight" program for the Presbyterian Homes community of Inver Grove Heights, MN. Marin hosted *The Spirit of People* radio talk show for five years, airing weekly and running simultaneously on the web. This platform offered her the opportunity to give a voice to all forms of healing and represent practitioners and teachers across the globe. She has sponsored bi-annual gatherings that brought together like minds, allowing them to network and support each other in their work. Marin is also an Inter-Spiritual Communicator and serves as a Life Coach, assisting others personally and guiding them with the tools they need to establish a

spiritual foundation and direction in their life. Marin resides in Hastings, Minnesota with her husband and two daughters.

https://www.facebook.com/FreeWillMagnified
http://www.freewillmagnified.com

Meet Cindy Halley, *The GODpillow* Lady

ONE DAY, MUCH TO my surprise, I woke up in the middle of my life and asked myself, "How did I get here?" Have you ever asked yourself the same question? I know what I was doing each day, but I wasn't aware of how I lived my life and how that affected me – and everyone else. I remember clearly looking around (as if to find the answer written down somewhere). I told myself that I was a "smart girl," but, somehow, everything was messed up. And I was clueless. This is not the life I planned.

Life always moved quickly for me, and I liked it like that. The quickness and speed by which I lived my life was exciting, spontaneous and never allowed me to evaluate how I was doing. My goal was to keep moving on to bigger and better things. And if that situation didn't work, well, I would always find another, better plan...(not really taking the time to sit and think about any consequence). If I made bad decisions, what the hell — tomorrow would be a better day. If I lost a job, I could always get a new one — tomorrow would be better day.

Anyone would be lucky to have me. I worked hard and I played hard; I was a survivor. Heck! If you knew what I had to go through, you probably would have given me a medal, too! And that is truly what I thought. The life I was living was for having fun — and who wouldn't want that?

I thought I deserved that attitude of "this is my time." I can do whatever and whomever I want. I was slim, attractive, educated and fun! But when the party was over, and the people were gone, I was left with a..."lacking" feeling. In fact, if I thought about it, I was sad. In fact, if I really looked at myself, I would cry, because I felt alone, isolated and unloved. I needed more fun and more people around. Who wants to be around someone who has depressed thoughts or feelings? I wasn't aware that I was living a double life: one that I would show other people, and the other for when I was alone. This worked for a long time...but on that day, the day when I woke up, it stopped working.

What stopped working was the "numbing effect" of drinking and all the partying? Having a couple of drinks or smoking a little pot kept me mellow, because I was high energy — and that was the story I told myself. In fact, I believed most of the stories I told myself — and if one didn't work, I would make up another story. That pattern lasted a long time. So I was constantly telling myself stories about my life. I had to believe them, because if I didn't believe them, how were the people around me going to believe them?

They may even see through me and see the real me — and I couldn't afford that. Inevitably, some people did see me, and what was happening, and that scared me! I knew that when they actually saw the "bullshit," I got "the look." Have you ever seen the look? It's the nonverbal message expressing disdain, disappointment and disapproval. Those were the worst feelings. It felt like I was turned inside out, plummeting in a downward spiral into my acidic, aching stomach. And, in one instant — composure. I found myself once again saying, "It's not that bad; tomorrow will be better. I promise!" But I knew deep down that I couldn't keep that promise. It wasn't going to be better. It would be even worse if I didn't numb myself again. That was the secret I kept. I knew I couldn't stop. I didn't stop earlier because of the pain from my past. Now I couldn't stop because the drinking and drugs took hold of me. I now needed to drink — but I didn't want to drink.

This is what we call the "jumping off place." You can't go back and it's hard to go forward. I know now that there is no problem in the world that doesn't have a Spiritual Solution, but at first that didn't sit right with me. I was raised Catholic, and that sounded religious! That "God thing" worked for others, but God left me a long time ago. I took the leap anyway! I had no problem leaping. Hey, in my past I was always leaping from one thing to another. But I knew I didn't have a grasp on this one. By the grace of God, I found the solution to help me look at things a little differently. I was willing, but I was also afraid.

I didn't realize how much of a fearful, unaware life I was living until I actually looked at myself. I was fearful of the pain of the past that always haunted me, so I drank to silence the memories. Before I could even look back, I had to lay a good foundation for myself.

Addiction is any container that holds your spirit. It could be alcohol, drugs, shopping, sex, Facebook, reading, television – anything that keeps you separated from your spirit and living the life of your dreams.

I was willing to admit that drinking was just a symptom of my problems. I knew my life was a little messy, but I never thought it was unmanageable, or that I had insane thinking! In time, I came to realize that the "story" of "it's not so bad" was coming from my ego. My ego had to be smashed. I was doing the same thing over and over again and expecting different results — and that is INSANE. So I surrendered my old way of thinking and learned "acceptance" — with a new perspective. This was the key, to learn to look at life and myself, to see exactly what is for the way it is. Especially not the way I wanted it to be or how I thought is should be. I acknowledged that I had a physical allergy, mental immaturity and was spiritually bankrupt.

I knew in my heart of hearts that I couldn't do this alone. But I didn't know where or how to start! It was suggested that I get on my knees and ask "the God of my understanding" to remove the obsession. I resisted that...but one day I was struggling so badly with the obsession to drink that in the middle of the afternoon, in the middle of my living room, I broke down, as desperate as can be! I remember that pivotal moment saying, "God take this from me."

Time stood still. I really can't remember how much time passed, but to my surprise, I felt relief! I really felt it! And at that moment, I "owned" the experience that God touched me and was listening. This truly was one of my Spiritual Transformations! Every time I surrender, a door opens and I know God is listening. I know I have to listen, as well. Since developing a relationship with GOD, I now take time in the morning to get on my knees (or you can sit and meditate) and ask God to direct me during the day. And every time I ASK, I find my day runs smoother.

That experience gave me the hope and courage to continue on my journey. My journey had to start in the past — not in the future of tomorrows. And there I found my "childhood victim" — and victims don't recover! I discovered that you could rewrite your past. I went back as an adult with new eyes and looked at my life, like the ghost of Christmas past. I saw a lonely little girl who thought she was abandoned, unloved and alone, living in a hopeless environment. I now had the wonderful opportunity to save her!

I embraced her and revealed a clear and detailed account of the surrounding circumstances. (Today as a loving reminder, I carry a picture of myself, as a 3 year old.) I now know that life isn't perfect, that people aren't perfect, and that I had a "supporting role" to impact those imperfect people — and I learned forgiveness, the ability to let go of any hope of a better past.

GOD was with me all along. He gave me the gift of perseverance, emotional honesty and a pursuit of independent thinking — and most of all, the gift of comedic relief. I was, and am, a child of GOD. I just forgot. I do not want to shut the door to those experiences, because it has created the person I am today. I have a new freedom, a new happiness and a strong determination to be the best version of myself, with the help of a loving GOD. I do my best, I show up and I serve with gratitude. I may not know what the next right thing is, but I know I can do the next thing right. I do my best.

My best is different on different days, and that is okay! It is spiritual progress, rather that spiritual perfection. I do not strive for perfection, because that is unattainable, but I keep striving! And when old character defects pop up, I recognize them for what they are — old fears manifesting with different faces. Today, I can pause, be still and experience the healing possibilities that come from prayer and meditation. As a result, I get the answers that I already knew I had within. More will be revealed when I am ready, when all is aligned just the way it should be! But the best part is at the end of my day. I get on my knees and say, "Thank you," for life is bountiful. I am ever reminding myself, "I am an instrument of GOD, with infinite love and joy."

And as I continue on my journey, I realize that my mission all along has been to share myself with others the gifts that I've received. Do you believe that you have the answers available to you? Are you willing to be open and honest with yourself? So here we are, inspired and knowing that great things, will happen. Are you ready?

In the Spirit of the Light,

Non-believers welcomed!

 Cindy Halley, aka The GODpillow Lady, has an entertaining style and speaks at workshops and expos around the country, sharing her own recovery. Her experience has led to the creation and expansion of her inspirational line of products to create one's sacred space. Cindy founded GODpillow through her recovery process nine years ago. The company is the result of Cindy's desire to develop a personal tool to use in building a successful approach for any long-term recovery. GODpillow is an inspirational reminder for positive change by realigning the physical with the spiritual. Her products are designed for you to create a balance between body, mind and spirit as you shift your focus to healing. Since 2003, the "GODpillow Family" has grown to more than 5,000 members in 10 countries, embroidered in four different languages, and is growing. GODpillow Products can be found in more than 35 treatment centers and select retail stores.

https://www.facebook.com/GODpillowLady
Visit www.godpillow.com

Meet Dennis Merritt Jones

Creating Conscious Relationships:
The Tapestry of a Life Worth Living

LIFE IS A TRIP we're not meant to travel alone. If we stop and consider our life's journey, we shall see that we entered into a lifetime of relationships beginning the moment we were born. From our birth mother, followed by other family members, and literally every other person we have encountered along the way has been connected like a string of pearls on one single invisible silver thread called relationship.

Like many others who spend more than a little time at the computer, I've also been pulled into the vortex of the Facebook phenomena where I have had an opportunity to experience what relationship means in a new way. Facebook, as an online social networking website, allows individuals anywhere on the planet to connect with old and new friends. When I say new friends, I mean *a whole lot* of new friends. There are currently over 900 million users on Facebook and it's growing daily. One of my computer geek friends refers to it as "viral" because its popularity has spread so quickly. Even my 91-year-old dad managed to get on board and now, between Skype and Facebook, he's making new friends all around the country and loving the opportunities it presents.

The question that arises for me is, what is it that makes Facebook (and other such websites) so compelling for so many people? No doubt, there are many people who are using Facebook for business networking. The Internet is the way of the future for marketing one's products and services; however, I believe it goes far beyond that. I believe Facebook is such a popular phenomena because people are hungry for connection. Every person desires relationship—where someone is there to witness his or her life. People want to know that who they are matters and that their presence on the planet makes a difference. Who among us does not long to be acknowledged, appreciated, well-received and supported by others? Facebook offers an amazing forum by means of which that realization may be achieved, not only with ease but also in a fun way.

When the topic of relationships come up most of us immediately think "significant other" relationships because that is where we invest a majority of our time. However, when we pause and consider the many other people we connect with on a daily basis we'll see that our lives are filled with relationships. For me, the realization is that without all of those relationships life would be meaningless:

From the strangers with whom I chat while standing "in line" at the market and my Facebook community with whom I chat "online," and my neighbors and colleagues, to my most beloved wife and family members (including my dog Mac); without them I would not want to be here--without those relationships life would be hollow. Metaphorically speaking, while life itself is the ultimate gift from the Creator, relationships are how the gift is woven into the tapestry of a life worth living; each separate thread, when combined with the others, adds a color, richness and dimension to life that we could never experience without them.

We are each driven by a deep urge to form an intimate connection with the world around us and most of us do this through relationships. If you take a soul look at this, you will see that your need for relationship actually stems from your basic human need to overcome your earthly sense of separation.

—Caroline Reynolds, *Spiritual Fitness*

As my friend Caroline Reynolds stated above, I too believe there is a spiritual component to this desire for connection, even if we are not consciously aware of its presence: Something quite extraordinary happens between ourselves and others when our lives intersect at the soul level. Be it a friend or significant other, when we consciously interface with those with whom we are in relationship we are connecting not with just a physical body, a personality or a name--we are connecting with the very essence of life--with the energy of joy, love, satisfaction and peace that comes in knowing we are not alone on our journey.

To share our journey with others is what life is really all about; that's why there is more than one of us on the planet. I have long defined "Relation-Ship" as a vessel in which two or more souls journey toward a common destination; the realization of our oneness in Life. This is where the journey and the destination really become one in the same as all pretense and sense of separation fall away, revealing what is real: the sacred space where who we are spills into each other's "being."

Unless we live isolated and alone at the top of a mountain, not having relationships is *not* an option; from the moment our feet hit the floor in the morning we enter into a continuum of relationships, beginning with the face we see staring back at us in the mirror. So, it's not a matter of *if* we will have relationships -- it's a question of *how conscious* shall we be in them. How mindfully awake we are in our relationships, determines if or not they will become authentic friendships. The level of our awareness and intention also determines what we shall bring to, and receive from, those relationships. The poet and artist Flavia said something profound about relationships when he wrote:

Some people come into our lives and quickly go. Some people stay for a while, and give us a deeper understanding of what is truly important in this life. They touch our souls...we gain strength from the footprints they have left on our hearts and we will never be the same.

In other words, every relationship we have, from our significant others, family and friends, to our neighbors and coworkers, and even the occasional stranger we allow into our lives, all bear something in common: Each will leave "footprints" on our hearts, as we will on theirs. Those footprints may leave a positive or, in some cases, negative impression but, in either case, each relationship brings with it, if we are conscious and teachable, an opportunity to learn more about our authentic selves and the role each person in our life plays in shaping who it is we have come to earth to be.

What does it mean to be conscious in our relationships? To be conscious in our relationships means to be mindfully present in the moment, fully engaged, and invested in bringing the highest and best of ourselves to the relationship while, at the same time, creating space for others to do the same; the challenging part of the practice includes remaining unattached as to if, how or when they shall do so. Not to worry--if you are indeed in a conscious relationship it will happen organically as it should. It can take time to create a conscious relationship but it all begins with open, honest, transparent communication. This doesn't usually happen by accident--it requires an intention to create a safe place where each person is supported in being who he or she really are. That is what makes it a conscious, authentic relationship--being real.

The takeaway for me is this: Conscious relationships matter because the more conscious and spiritually grounded we are in our relationships the more authentic (or real) they become. Authenticity is the passageway leading directly to the soul. Is it possible to have truly authentic relationships wherein we can be who we really are and, at the same time, create space for others to be who they really are? I propose that it is not only possible, but it will become the norm for any person who is willing to make the commitment to do the work. Our relationships are the vehicles for our evolution as individuals and a species. If we are fully conscious, our relationships offer us the clearest view of our own souls because they invite us to look directly into the face of the Beloved One and see our own reflection. We have come here to have relationships: From the cradle to the grave and all along the way in between, it is the relationships we have on the journey that truly make life worth living, so why not make the journey consciously?

Baseball legend Ty Cobb once wrote, "If I had the chance to live my life over, I'd do things a little different...I'd have more friends." His wisdom is sage: I don't want to wait until the end of my life to understand the importance and meaning of having shared my life in authentic relationships with true friends; it's the journey we take *together* that matters most, not the destination. What I know is that every new friendship offers us another opportunity to build a bridge to a person's heart and soul, which, in turn, reminds us that we are never alone as long as the bridge is maintained. Perhaps even more important, with every authentic friendship comes the opportunity to witness the greatness of whom that person really is and, in the process, be reminded that we wouldn't be able to see it in him or her if it didn't also live within us.

At the end of the day, relationships really are what it's all about, isn't it? Value your relationships, treasure your friendships and don't take them for granted because each one is a rich reminder of how blessed you are--your friendships truly are, to a large extent, the tapestry of your life. If you are currently on Facebook and we have not yet connected, lets do so. The journey is far too good not to share it with like-minded souls! I would be honored to add you to the tapestry of my life.

Peace,
Dennis Merritt Jones

Throughout his lifetime, award winning author Dennis Merritt Jones has been on a quest to inspire and lift people to a higher expression of life. His personal vision is to guide people to their purpose, knowing that when a person fully awakens to who they are and why they are on the planet, they begin to naturally share their gift with humankind and, in the process, create an enriching life for themselves and the world around them. Dennis' most recent book, *The Art of Uncertainty ~ How to Live in the Mystery of Life and Love It,* was recently the recipient of the Nautilus Silver Award designed to highlight books that offer new ideas and options for a better world for everyone. In addition or being a keynote speaker, respected teacher, spiritual mentor and consultant, Dennis is also a columnist for print media as well as the Huffington Post. Dennis believes that there is a new consciousness of unity, cooperation and reverence rising in humankind where the value of all life is considered sacred.

www.facebook.com/DennisMerrittJones
www.DennisMerrittJones.com

Meet Narda Mohammed of *We Are All One*

MY PERSONAL JOURNEY OF inspiration and spiritual enlightenment began at the age of 25 after reading the book, The Secret. The message of The Secret resonated with me in such a profound way; it validated what I silently thought and felt, but never expressed. This one message triggered great change in my life, though at that point, I had no idea what was about to take place. Everything that was "normal" slowly, but surely, began to be removed, adjusted or transformed in my life. I entered a completely new place of self-realization and self-creativity in which I began taking charge of my personal divine power. This huge life transformation brought with it many interesting, mind-blowing and beautiful experiences, some of which may be unbelievable to most. I consciously stepped out of the life I knew, that labeled box of what was stamped upon me and expected of me since being born and raised on a small Caribbean island. I stepped into the unknown, having to be in a place of complete trust in each and every moment, being

in the divine flow of well-being that has brought me to this now moment, sharing with you, beautiful being, my personal story.

For as long as I can remember, I always knew I wanted to live my life in service, helping others realize their true potential and power, to inspire and motivate them into a place of ultimate joy and happiness — and help them understand they can have a fruitful and blissful life, despite anything they may have endured up to this moment in life. I deliberately stepped into my heart's desire in early 2010 when I finally decided to follow my dreams, to begin helping people. I became a Life Coach. By far, this was one of the most joyous decisions I had ever made in my life. Little did I know then, that something huge was about to come my way, something unexpected and life altering. Later that year, I was presented with what I now call a blessing in disguise, an event that triggered huge transformation in my life and took me down a path I never for one second thought was even possible; I never thought one's life can even be transformed in the way that mine did.

In the summer of 2010, I had a hand injury that seemed quite simple, but ultimately was an unexpected hardship; two hand surgeries left me out of work and financially paralyzed. At this time, while building my life coaching business, I was unable to do the job that paid my bills — and what resulted was an influx of emotions and frustrations. Little did I know then that my life was about to be turned upside down and emptied? The very core of my "being-ness" and who I thought I was would be challenged and dispelled, and the structures of my own belief and emotional systems were about to shatter. And emerging from the depths of my soul would be a powerful being who can stand before the world in my individual beautiful and loving truth.

This period that I like to refer to as my spiritual awakening was so unlike anything I ever thought I would've ever experienced in my life. I experienced dark moments in which

I was unable to see a single glimpse of light; I literally felt consumed with darkness. These were times of great loneliness and sadness, times when I questioned everything, even my purpose here on earth. So many thoughts were running through my head that I was unable to sleep for a several days in a row. It was quite a journey — a journey back to my true divine self. Back then, I had no idea all those experiences would have brought me this far, with the level of understanding that I now have, with great appreciation for everyone and everything. Who would've known that from such darkness, such great light can emerge. When we're in a place of darkness, we forget that for all the darkness we experience, so too can we experience the same measure of light. The further back we are pulled into the darkness, the further forward into the light we are propelled. This is called the rubber band effect.

Christmas 2010 was one of the darkest times I have ever experienced, second only to my mom's death when I was 8 years old. It was in this dark time in late December that a beautiful angel gently glided into my awareness and gifted me with an intuitive energy healing session, one that left me in such awe and appreciation; I wanted to give to others that exact experience and feeling that was given to me. This ignited a desire within me to expand my education and learn about the field of Reiki energy healing, which I pursued shortly thereafter. My healing work with others opened me up to even greater healing within myself, which then led me to further study in the field of hypnosis. I became certified as a Clinical Hypnotist. I was highly inspired to study hypnosis to better help my clients heal, for I understood the power of one's thinking and a person's belief systems through my own personal and professional experiences. A person can want as much as he or she wants, but if that person doesn't believe that he or she can have it or experience it, then they won't. It always comes back to your belief system, your dominant thought patterns and the energy that you attach to what you want or don't want.

My journey of self-expansion and service to others sped up at such a rate that what may have taken another person years to learn took me months. I truly believe part of the grand divine plan for my life was the Divine/The Universe/God saying, "Get to work, Narda."

One of the greatest lessons I learned during this time was to surrender the complete process to the Divine, to be okay with however and whenever things will unfold, even beyond my own imagination. It was during one of these great moments of surrender in my life, a time when I could've reacted to a situation but did not, when I was inspired to create a Facebook page called "We Are All One." It profoundly occurred to me that the message of Oneness — that we are one from one Divine source, regardless of what name we may choose to call the Divine/God

— needed to be sent out into the world. For we are not as separate, or even as different, from each other as the way we may have been taught to believe. Know this: Beyond each physical garment/exterior/body lies a pure Divine being, a soul that is connected to all of creation. In true essence, we are all one. When the people of the world see all life forms as one with themselves — and know that what we do to others, we do to ourselves — and then we will all live in a space of complete loving kindness and unity with each other and all things.

Since the creation of my page, "We Are All One," in June 2011, the page has received thousands of Likes from across the world, from people representing every walk of life, culture, religion, etc. — those who, in some way, if not entirely, resonate with the term "We're all one." This page has been a source of inspiration and edification on many levels to those who have sought out its content.

I have met and interacted with many beautiful souls because of the We Are All One page. One, in particular, is an amazing soul who has helped me tremendously along my own path, as a friend and teacher. She is Britny Lopez, my business partner and co-owner of our company, The Beautiful Unfolding. It always amazes me how the Universe connects people. In mid-2011 when We Are All One was just launched, Britny also paid attention and listened to the call from Divine to create a Facebook page called "We Are All One." Soon she realized that such a page already existed — the one I created — and we first interacted and connected on this beautiful, illuminating path.

Some other Facebook pages that I have created — which also have touched thousands of lives — are Divine Evolution, Divine Energy and Health Remedies. These pages inspire and educate others on spiritual and health matters.

My life and spiritual path, thus far, have been an amazing ride and a beautiful unfolding, nothing like what I would've imagined for myself, with continuous learning, growth and expansion. This journey has brought me to a place of complete heart-centeredness, where I now rest in total surrender, belief, trust and allowance in The Universe/Divine/God.

It is my greatest passion to help others learn how to heal their past, joyously move forward in the present, and enjoy a blissful and fruitful future. I do believe that most people are unaware that this is even possible, that they can come to a place of healing with what was done to them or what they may have done. And yet, it is possible. You can have a life greater than anything you can imagine for yourself, once you allow the Divine to help you on your path. Life was not meant to be a suffering journey, but one of learning, enjoyment and enlightenment. There are no mistakes — only lessons that cause you to expand. No experience is in vain; each experience can be used for your benefit.

Despite what you may have experienced in the past, you can mentally and emotionally travel back into time, using the wisdom and knowledge that you now possess, and look at any given situation from a different point of view. You can shift your perspective and now grab hold of something positive, a lesson of some sort from that very situation that was left dormant in your memory or emotions. You can benefit from past situations, whether they were negative or positive. You may not be able to change the events of the past, but you can change how you now view them. Despite whatever you may have done or was done to you, you can have a fulfilling life. You are not marked or doomed by the past. The present and future is yours for the taking. The decision in this present moment is whatever you truly want — and the power is always yours. Whether you choose to consciously seize that power, or silently hand it to someone or a situation, is totally up to you. The choice is always yours.

It is truly a joy and honor to be in this present moment, having shared with you my personal story. The Divine within me honors and celebrates the Divine within you.

Narda Mohammed was born and raised in the Caribbean, endured many personal challenges and experienced an interesting spiritual journey, what she refers to as a "wake-up call" that led to a spiritual awakening that took her down an unconventional career path at a young age. Now residing in the USA, she is a Clinical Hypnotist,

Life Coach, Energy Healer, Author and Motivational Speaker. Narda's passion is to help motivate, inspire and educate others that they can heal their past, change their lives positively and live an enriching, fruitful life despite whatever they may have experienced and endured. Visit Narda's webpage, *We Are All One - https://www.facebook.com/#!/We.Are.All.One.*

http://www.nardamohammed.com

Meet Britny Lopez of *The Beautiful Unfolding*

I BELIEVE THAT SOMETIMES we know exactly what we are here to do from the very beginning. I believe that as soon as words begin to come out of the mouths of some souls, they are perfectly orchestrated and they just know what they are here to say. That happens to be the case for me. When I was a child, I always knew that I had a message. As a very young child, I began writing speeches and began telling the world what I thought was truth. I frequently asked my mother, "When am I going to be a 'people'?" I meant adult, but "people" was my 3-year-old mind's interpretation of adult, or better yet, "important." My mom always responded with, "You ARE a people, you're a person, too!" "No," I replied, "I mean a big people, like you." You can just feel "the yearn" in my young words. I wanted to make an impact; I wanted my words to matter. I knew that there was a difference and I couldn't wait until there wasn't.

The first speech I ever wrote was in the first grade. My teacher entered me into a contest to write a speech on the topic of "Equality." Surprisingly, I ended up winning that contest. My mother was a strong advocate of equality, and I was frequently told that everyone was essentially "the same." She explained to me that all people were the same, even if we all look differently. She told me that a person can be black, white, purple or polka-dotted — infinite possibilities — but we are all the same. Everyone should be treated with that in mind. I took that to heart. I believe that. I guess that is why I was able to conjure the passion and understanding when I was 6. It was easy for me to understand when my mom said it. It was simple. I understand why I understood equality as a first grader. I suppose this is the beginning of my understanding that "we are all one" and my true belief in the Golden Rule.

As you have gathered, I entered life with an advantage: I was blessed with a great mother. She taught me how important it is to be kind and listen to everyone. Her heart has always been with the sick, the elderly and the homeless. My mother instilled true love and compassion in my brothers and me. I believe that is so important. My mother taught me according to what I was ready to learn — I learned quickly, and I was able to retain the information. That continues to be the theme in my life.

As a child, I thoroughly enjoyed being asked the question, "What do you want to be when you grew up?" Not only did I have an answer, but I believed that I would fulfill my desires one day. My answer was always, "I am going to be a teacher, doctor, artist and dancer/singer." Explaining that dancing and singing were more of what I would do for fun, they were just added in. But I meant what I said. There was a magical, gentle knowing within me. I figured that if what my mom said is true, "You can be anything you want to be" and I chose to be all of those, then I could be all of those. What's great is that I happen to express myself in all of those exciting ways in my life right now! I had good reason to believe in those desires, because I am lucky and privileged enough to say that those are my life purpose and I have already begun working on them.

My spiritual awakening began when I was about age 19. I thought I was so spiritual at that point. I loved Jesus. I loved anything old and sacred — crystals, art, creating, love, animals, nature, adventure and freedom. I remembered what I was reading. I remembered all that I learned. I even knew what I was gravitating toward. I was studying some important concepts: A Course in Miracles, Louise Hay, and The Four Agreements. The Bible — all good things to be reading at my age, or at any age, actually. I remember walking into the bookstore and a seeing a small, red book on the bookshelf, right at the front of the store. Oprah's bestseller, it said, and it caught my attention.

It was supposed to hold the secret to getting all that you desire. At that point in my life, I was totally open to receiving "The Secret." I totally wanted the magic formula to receiving peace of mind and making all of my dreams come true. It thrilled me. Right away I decided to manifest everything that I wanted.

I went after a high-paying job, a car, a relationship. I blew myself away at how I manifested so much, so quickly. I manifested an amazing job with amazing salary and an amazing location, as well as perfect co-workers. I manifested a passionate relationship. I manifested everything I asked for — yet, my subconscious vibration was attracting experiences that were just as challenging to me. My life was built up, only to crumble down one way or another.

Somehow, some way, I began using The Secret to manifest challenging relationships and lower-paying jobs. Trust me, you do NOT want the formula to this. My jobs were always in alignment with something that I cared about, but the pay and the stress levels were not what I intended. And my relationships were a lot of things, but healthy was not one of them.

At that point, I had no idea what true love even was — and I don't think I even realized that I should have cared about how I was being treated. I was too focused on the giving aspect of love that I forgot I was supposed to be treated a certain way in return. When I love, I love with "my everything," and I truly want that person to feel the love I have for them. I am very clear about how I feel. I was confronted with a situation in which no matter how much love I gave, it wasn't the right kind of love, or I wasn't what they wanted anymore, and now they wanted something completely different.

Or, to make matters worst, they wanted me and something else at the same time. In a mature relationship, this is when one adult begins speaking in calm and composed manner and expresses love, and his or her desires, to another adult who hears, acknowledges and takes into consideration the other adult's feelings. We, however, were not adults.

We handled it the way any two whiny 20-year-old kids handled money problems and relationship stress: by eating hot dogs and drinking cheap wine ... 'Lots and lots of both. We also spent our time creating masterpieces out of our frustration. The art we created was lovely. But just like in any other life, sometimes we woke up on the sunny side of the wine bed, and other times, we didn't. We both had bad attitudes and we both felt we had our reasons. I am sure we did, but our reasons didn't bring us any closer to resolution. We needed to separate, learn, and most importantly, heal. We needed to grow up!

When this relationship unraveled, I began to get interested in meditation; soon I began meditating daily. I noticed an immediate shift in my moods, as well as my creative impulses. All of a sudden, I had creativity flowing through me. I had motivation to get my art supplies out and actually use them. It had been a while since that had happened. I began expressing myself again. This felt so good. And up to this point in my life, I had never encountered anything that could better express how I felt quite like the arts. I was having great insight regarding fresh, organic foods — and veggies in particular. It felt like an epiphany when I began integrating all of it into my life. I felt so vibrant and alive — so healthy and present. Plus, the foods were delicious when I cooked them properly.

At the beginning of 2010, I received a nudge to attend a conference — and to see a specific intuitive. I was very excited to speak to this psychic to learn about my situation. I saw that I could get my aura picture taken, so I stood in line; soon, a nice gentleman asked me to come over to his table. He told me that he sensed that I had been having difficulty speaking my truth. He then guided me to have my aura picture taken. I had seen other aura photos of people at the event, but when I saw my energy picture, I knew it truly was mine. I felt an instant connection to it. A woman at booth interpreted my aura picture. She said I am a "Spiritual Teacher" here to speak and teach. I'm also an entrepreneur and a natural, intuitive leader. That resonated with me, but I was not aware of my spiritual wisdom, let alone something that I could teach! That fascinated me.

Before long, I was meeting with the intuitive who had initially attracted my attention. I sat in her booth and noted that she was adorable. She was a sweet, little Indian woman, a Vedic Psychic. She said she also was a healer. She looked at me intently. She pulled some cards from a deck and then asked to see my hands. She took them within hers, and her eyes widened. She lightly gasped. And then she said, "You're a healer." My mom happened to be with me, thank God, because I doubt anyone would have believed me without her confirmation. Imagine being 23 years of age and having someone tell you that you are a physical and emotional healer. It was quite a shock, I assure you. It's funny, too, because in some odd way it felt right. I knew what she was saying was true.

I left that conference shocked and invigorated. I felt like I sort of knew what I was doing on this Earth. I felt to some degree I was placed on this planet because I heal people and I teach people. I would personally add that I love people. I didn't really know where this understanding would lead, but I knew I was headed in the right direction. I did a lot of reading and research at this time. I meditated A LOT. I sent healing in my own way to where I knew it was needed.

Since then, I have had multiple life-changing experiences and many healings have taken place. I have been on this journey of awakening with the curiosity of a child and the intricate nature of a scientist. I am always learning and expanding and sharing what I learn with everyone I meet. I had a situation in which I randomly ended up in the middle of the Mojave Desert without a car. I was shocked to find myself in such a remote place and with no one that I knew within an hour of me. But in retrospect, it really allowed me time to think...reflect.... heal...and solidify my understanding of "me." I meditated. I healed. I talked. I healed. This time in my life was such an important healing, cleansing, purifying experience. I had no luck in finding a paying job in my field of interest, so I had to figure out how to combine my passions with my ability to support myself. I needed to eat, buy toilet paper, pay my rent. I really had to surrender over to a higher plan and go with the flow.

I knew that if I were supposed to have a job, I would have had one. I knew that there was a reason why I was at home...healing...and examining the whole process in this way. I literally knew every detail, and I understood why it was happening. I believe that my journey has allowed me to step into being a teacher about awakening, and much more. Moving forward on our life purpose. Tapping into our passions and moving forward on them no matter what. Being true to you, without compromise. Listening to the intuition within. Taking the action steps as you feel guided. Trusting the whole thing as it unfolds. Loving and appreciating Self and Divine. Knowing that it all has purpose.

The Beautiful Unfolding just sort of "happened." I was pondering the idea that life is unfolding perfectly, and as I was sitting in my workspace one day, the words "The Beautiful Unfolding" popped into my mind. I loved the sentiment! I just loved it! I took a deep breath, closed my eyes, and the Facebook logo popped up in my mind. I concluded that I was to make a Facebook page called "The Beautiful Unfolding." To manifest that, I just went with the flow, paying attention to nudges that felt important, taking action when guided. The whole thing just took shape.

As I cared for my fledgling Facebook page, I was taken under the wings of many other pages, and they helped gather my following. And on my page, I shared the guidance I was receiving, and I created a place where people could buy readings, guidance and healing. I was being fueled by the experience, and the fans were becoming more than fans; they were becoming friends and students. The connections and love made on The Beautiful Unfolding has been my favorite part.

Eventually I connected with the woman who would become my business partner, Narda Mohammed. Narda was the administrator and owner of the Facebook page, "We are All One." At the time, she was seeking guidance on how to connect with the angelic realm and general information on the spiritual path. I loved the idea of teaching people about the angels and how to connect with them and how their messages come through. I began teaching, and it was a tremendous success. I began to realize that the class I just pulled together was actually having a great impact on people's lives. They were leaving the experience in a better, more peaceful space. Their entire lives were different.

When I am teaching the many courses that The Beautiful Unfolding offers, I am in "my element." It is where I belong. I was put here to teach people about their intuition, meditation, natural health, energy, healing, and life purpose, among many other things. Something surges through me when I teach. I trust and believe in the process. I am beginning to see that everything truly unfolds beautifully when you go with the flow. When you surrender, flow and allow, that is when magic happens. I love magical unfolding's. I love the feeling of a miracle realized. Even more so, I love the feeling of watching someone else feel the feeling of a miracle realized. Ahhh, this life is definitely my favorite.

Britny Lopez, this laid-back, yet profound, spiritual teacher who was born and raised in Los Angeles, California, is pioneering spiritual courses for modern women, including for those who resonate with Indigo and Crystal energy. She has a passion for offering personalized assistance and courses to light workers, intuitive(s), healers, teachers and those who are seeking more love and their true life's purpose. She is able to help you find what it is next to be healed in a fun and practical way! And move forward! Isn't that what we really want? Find her at *www.thebeautifulunfolding.com*

http://www.facebook.com/TheBeautifulUnfolding

Meet Kathy Johnson of *Protech Consulting Group*

MY LIFE HAS BEEN ONE of highs and lows, happy and sad, ill and well and now I find myself in a place that consists of all these energies. In the years between the 1980 & 90's I was in what I call the high tide of my life, I was Vice President of Sales with a national fundraising publishing company, earning a six figure income, happily married, had just given birth to my son, wonderful friends and in all areas my life was good.

In the mid 90's my husband and I divorced after many years of marriage, and within two years after my divorce life was nothing like the life I had been living. I left my job and accepted another job that required some travel, and right before my big break in my career instead I receive a big break but not in my career in my physical condition. I was involved in a car accident that leads to several years of physical struggles with my health. I find myself involved in a series of surgeries, which left me debilitated, and in severe pain. In less than five years, I went from living the life I love to wondering what kind of life I would have left.

Next would bring with it the struggle to qualify for disability, it was hard to fathom that I would even be contemplating social security disability but that was my only option. I was not able to work my mind was as sharp as ever but my body was no longer employable. I never thought my life would be in the position I found myself in.

For ten years, my life consisted of living on pain pills, doctor visits, surgeries, failed relationships, and financial hardships. I was imprisoned in a world where four walls and loneliness were all I knew, friends rarely came, my son grew up and started a life of his own family members passed away, and all I had left were the painful memories of the life I loved but no longer lived. Everything happens for a reason I have always believed that. This journey has taken me to places I have never been. Perhaps I was meant to go there in order that I would understand how to help others, as well help myself. I had no suffering such as this before. I have called on GOD many times in my past when I was going through horrific times. Nothing I had ever experienced would prepare me for GOD'S intervention when I was ready for change.

I realized I am meant to be where I was at that time I have no doubt, that I feel this. At the beginning of doing this, I began thinking more about GOD, and asking questions, and I will say in all truth that I did indeed...receive answers, within my heart. The journey, I believe was to renew my faith...and it has! I will not claim to be here at this moment in time other than to do GOD'S work. I realized that GOD does not work in mysterious ways unless you think he is a mystery. I knew what my purpose was and that was to show the truth about faith. You cannot deny psychology exists and using my skills from my past as well as my experiences in my present, I have developed a habit of positivity, which has brought me love, contentment and joy. In a world of accomplishments, with strife, stress and success this leaves many people wondering "is this as good as it gets", "if I were to die today what type of Legacy would I leave".

So there comes a time when we all realize that we are capable of more, doing more, accomplishing more, seeing more and producing more, it is then, that you find your purpose, and that is when I found mine. To know your purpose, is to know, understand, and accept yourself, without pretense and prejudice.

"Love is the answer and you know that for sure" John Lennon.

Finally, the day came when I had a revelation and decided I was sick and tired of being sick and tired as so many people often said. I started to pray and I prayed the prayer of faith not fear, I wanted free from the pills I had lived on for so long, the financial hardships I was having to endure, I wanted a dog a cat and a loving man. I wanted to start my life over again. One day a friend of mine introduced me to someone that would be the catalyst in propelling my life forward to the life I knew I wanted and deserved. I chose to be victorious over my circumstances. I realized I may have some physical limitations but my attitude was definitely something that was not crippled and with one decision to change, change came.

My new relationship with a wonderful man bought me to a new state, new neighborhood, a new house, a cat from the pound, and a precious dog that was found by a new friend on the side of the freeway that had been thrown out as I had felt so many times in the past. Now I have a happy family and each day I get back to the life that I love.

My one friend that has been there for years told me after I moved away that I had to get on face book so she and I could talk, and share pictures and keep up with each other. Before I knew it, I had a personal page and I loved it, then I found myself following her fan page and other fan pages and now more than being inspired and encouraged. I was meeting other people from all over the world and sharing with them. I was hooked! Face book was as good as any motivational seminar I had ever attended.

After a few months, my friend was adding a coaching division to her company and asked me if I would help her by helping some of her clients with their career decisions. I could coach them during their transitioning from losing their jobs, to helping them find their passion and purpose. Shortly I had my own fan page and Protech-Consulting Group was born. Now I was part of a global playground whereby I was sharing with others, posting my own original quotes and little by little regaining my ability that I thought I had lost long ago. I seemed to have found my place in society again.

As the universe had planned it, while coaching others, I used the Laws of Attraction processes, future vision work, meditating and positive thought empowerment coaching. This method helped to unleash the knowingness that each of us have in our Soul-Knowledge, that universal energy will successfully guide us to that which we seek. Whatever we desire... desires us, whatever we fear... manifest likewise each producing your bounty. We truly are what we think.

Utilizing the Laws of attraction is as easy as three steps:

1. Learn to *deliberately* choose your thoughts... (*Think*)

2. Learn to use *visualization* with real emotion to manifest your dreams. (*Feel*)

3. Use *appreciation* of all that surround you and allow good things to come to you (*Live*).

It was a real revelation when I realized that I could create my world with my thoughts! We live in a wonderful world, and through my coaching with Protech Consulting Group I am so happy to see that others are learning not just about the Laws of Attraction but how to utilize them in creating a world they love. When you pay attention to your thoughts emotions and feelings to create the life you want instead of using those same processes to create the life you do not want or more of what you do not want the road to happiness will be paved with Joy, Hope, and Reward instead of unhappiness, fear doubt, and worry.

For some people the idea of success revolves around money, or the acquisition of property or material possessions, and there was times in my life when I was right there myself. Now I consider a state of joy as the greatest achievement of success. I also find deep joy in having the power to live your ideal life by choosing powerful positive thoughts. (Face it... any thought that is positive is... powerful) l Once you understand that,

and add emotion to the thought, that is what you will bring to you...
AWESOMENESS.

I have seen this with my Face book fan page. Every post I share
shows me how my thoughts are transferred to others from the Likes,
Comments, and Shares from my face book fans. It cost nothing to share
positivity to the world, but it cost dearly to hold negativity in your mind.

I am in AWE with the universe today, I find myself often speechless,
and am left solely with my positive thought. ...You become what you
think about all day long...

So, catch a good vibe . . . spread it around . . . and watch what happens!

Until Next time . . . Much love and Blessings

Kathy Johnson

Kathy Johnson has more than twenty–five years of
experience in mid to executive business management.
She also excels in speaking, and writing and is about
to embark on a worldwide tour with the *A Course in
Courage Victory Tour.* Social media administration is
now a passion of hers and she thoroughly enjoys working with her subscribers through Protech Consulting Group. Ms. Johnson also spent
a significant amount of time participating in non-profit fundraising
for a homeless organization and home bound residents over the years.
Kathy truly enjoys contract negotiation for non-profits organizations,
also continues to work as a business consultant, and spent many a good
deal of her career, as Vice president of sales for national publishing company. Having also been a day care owner, she has learned to be flexible on
many levels within her professional and personal life.

https://www.facebook.com/protechcg
http://www.protechconsultinggroup.com

Meet Peter Canova of *Pope Annalisa*

My Journey with the Pope

LIFE IS MORE MAGICAL than you would ever believe, and the magic flows from within you. This is the lesson I learned in a decade long odyssey that transformed me from an international businessman to the author of a multi-award winning book about an abused African nun who rises to become the first female pope. I'm unique in this anthology in that:

I'm not a woman but a man writing about women.

Yet before this chapter ends, you will realize it is all about how the male is in the female and the female is in the male as both Karl Jung and the ancient spiritual texts told us. Before we speak of all that, however, I need to tell you a bit about *magic* and how the miraculous appears in our lives.

Of Magic and Men's Eyes

What is magic? It's not some event trumpeted by elves, fairies, angels, or even David Copperfield. There are no puffs of smoke or any flurry of Hollywood sound effects. It's not an external event at all, at least not in its inception. Magic happens when, by some means, the filters of our everyday consciousness get dislodged or even removed. We carry these filters inside us at a subconscious or even an unconscious level and they cloud our vision. Fear, anger, depression, despair, disbelief, and hurt are a few of the prisms through which the light of our lives gets bent and distorted.

Often these filters get dislodged when a person has hit the bottom of the barrel from a traumatic event—illness, accidents, death of a loved one, abuse—the cause doesn't matter, *it's the response to adversity that's important.* The theme of this book is inspiration, and inspiration is our primary tool for overcoming life's adversity. But you cannot overcome adversity from an ordinary, egoist, fearful state of consciousness. You must have *inspired* consciousness meaning that you must allow spirit *in-side* you.

When the filters of our ordinary consciousness are removed from the lens of our existence, when rationality and disbelief take a back seat to faith and letting go to a greater order in the universe, something magical happens. You probably won't notice it at first. It's like riding on a subway and the train makes a small, smooth transition to a different track. The change is small at the point of convergence but it becomes huge as the train moves on down the line. Then, one day, you step off the train and find yourself in a different space.

The Magic Kingdom

In a quantum leap, you've made a silent transition to a higher orbit of life. But what is this "magic?" What does that mean and how does it manifest and express itself? What happens when our "filters" recede into the background?

The most prominent feature of this new outlook is that your intuition comes to the fore even as your rational mind takes a back seat. No, you don't become irrational; you just don't let your rationality intrude on your natural intuitive experiences. When this transition happened to me, I could only liken it to a person sitting in front of a radio all his life and getting static.

But then one day, through persistence, faith, and nowhere else to turn, I happened upon a channel that came through loud and clear and it broadcasted 24/7. Like a guiding hand, it seemed to run a movie about my life, yet not a movie about what I was, more like a movie of where it wanted me to go. It happened through phenomena such as synchronicities, dreams, premonitions, and déjà vu. It heralded healing, direction, and sense of purpose in my life. But the best way to describe it is to tell my story and the story of Pope Annalisa, a woman who has come to be an inspiration for many people.

My Story Begins

Sometimes life seems to hit you from all sides. I went through a period when six out of the ten major causes of heart attacks hit me at once. It was like drowning at the bottom of a funnel down which several streams of toxic waste were being poured at once. Deaths in the family, strained relations with family members, business, and financial problems, and moving to a new location with no friends was bad enough but then my wife was diagnosed with a life threatening illness.

I was scared and depressed. I did have a spiritual orientation, but I was still like a bystander to a train wreck feeling helpless about how to support my wife. Yet the seeds of my salvation had already been sown without me realizing it. Just before my wife's diagnosis, I had been guided to take up writing. Though I was sinking in worry, I managed to conceive a story based on a challenge someone put to me. The challenge was to write about a concept no one else had addressed before, a tough task.

And it came to me that I would write a story about the first woman to become a pope. And I knew Mary Magdalene would play a major part in the story. And I knew these women would be abused, scorned, and discarded. And I knew they would rise again in triumph. And I didn't have a clue in hell where any of this was coming from.

A genre bending, epic story by a relatively inexperienced first-time, straight, white, male author writing from a woman's point of view was

the equivalent of literary suicide. It didn't matter. It was a burning obsession like a fever that had to work its way through my body. I compart-
mentalized all the negative reinforcement I received. I filed it away in
the maybe- it's- so- maybe- it's- not section of my brain library, and pro-
ceeded to channeled all my desperate energy into my book.

I have no doubt that my wife's ferocious courage in battling her illness was partly what inspired me, but years later I realized it was way
beyond that. The whole storyline was so alien to my life experience until
then. I knew nothing about Mary Magdalene, so why was I writing
about her? No one else knew anything about her either. Scant information was out there about this mysterious woman.

Annalisa's Story

Annalisa herself, like Mary Magdalene in my trilogy of books, was raped
and abused as a young woman. She was an outcast, and when through
a series of world-shaking circumstances this miraculous nun became
pope, she was hated, feared, and ridiculed by the male power structure
into which she had fallen like a blazing meteor.

Her papacy existed under the shadow of impending nuclear war.
Seemingly insurmountable forces lined up against her, blaming her for
the ills of their troubled world. They sought to eradicate her spirit and
her new vision of what it meant to be human. But she survived and tri-
umphed through all her hardships because her soul was centered in a
higher dimension inside herself.

She allowed her inner world of dreams, premonitions, and spiritual
guides to come forth. Moreover, she held them to be the *real* world. She
treated the outer world of turmoil as an *illusion*. She tapped into the
truth that we are all aspects of the divine slumbering in forgetfulness,
and if we cultivate the feminine faculties of heart felt intuition, imagination, and creativity it can steer us through the turbulent sea of life.

Cosmic Journey

Ultimately, I came to realize that the true story all along was not about
the personages of Mary Magdalene or Annalisa. These two women

symbolized the feminine archetype itself. It is a consciousness manifesting itself in ways that can transform us as human beings by transforming our ability to perceive reality with different eyes. I came to understand that I had been given a cosmic homework assignment to chronicle the resurgence of this intuitive energy once prevalent in early human societies when people lived closer to the rhythms of the earth. Their cultures nurtured the faculties of the goddess figures they once worshipped in the many Mystery Schools that dotted the ancient world. Learning about this feminine mystery was my given task.

And lo and behold, half way into the decade it took to finish my novel, an explosion of material on Mary Magdalene came cascading forth in books, over the internet, and even as topics of casual conversation. Tracing Magdalene's trail also led me to the alternative gospels of the suppressed Gnostic Christian mystics. In these texts Jesus teaches a hidden wisdom about opening the path to salvation from the troubles of the world:

"When you make the two into one, and when you make the inner as the outer, and the upper as the lower, and when you make male and female into a single one, so that the male shall not be male, and the female shall not be female: . . . then you will enter [the kingdom]."
—The Gospel of Thomas

Our left brain represents the male faculties of analysis, order, linear thinking, and status quo. Our right brain represents the female faculties of intuition, imagination, holistic thinking, and creativity. Our early ancestors once roamed the earth embraced in the womb of the feminine. To master our environment, humans left that womb and began using their male attributes. We've largely dwelled in this left-brain consciousness for ages now.

But two thousand years ago, Jesus told us the same thing psychologists like Jung and Maslow have told us in the modern age—we must integrate the fragmented parts of our male/female being into an operating harmony to become whole individuals capable of living life to its fullest. All along the true story was a grand movement of intuitive spiritual evolution pushing many others and me into an integrated consciousness. Flowing up that stream was what had guided me, a most unlikely candidate, to tell you the story contained in these Pages That Inspire.

I cannot guide you to the magic kingdom, that's your journey. I can only assure you from my experience that it is real. I gave you the testimony of my story and some hints how higher awareness may be contacted. What I can tell you for certain is that tapping into it saved both my wife and I. It launched us from the pit of despair into a fulfilling new direction in life.

The feminine energy of intuitive, heart-based perception is a rising tide, and it's moving all of us into balance. It is your hope, and it is your future. Its imaginative faculties will transform your ability to penetrate the higher dimensions from which you originated. And when you do, I think you will realize that we are the fingers of the divine touching the face of this world. Our purpose is to spiritualize the material while bringing the experience of the material back to spirit, for we are the bridge between the dimensions.

This is the exalted purpose of your being. Never give up hope. We all have a unique story to tell and a triumph to achieve. Please let my story and Annalisa's stand as testimony to this truth.

 Peter Canova has been an international businessman for over three decades. He is also a multi-award winning author and inspirational speaker. His book, Pope Annalisa (*popeannalisa.com*), has won nine national and international book awards. Peter is a leading expert on the Gnostic gospels, ancient spiritual traditions, and the implications of quantum physics. He is a columnist for Patheos, the interfaith website.

www.patheos.com
https://www.facebook.com/pages/POPE-ANNALISA/287558082643

Meet Kathleen O'Keefe-Kanavos of *Surviving Cancerland: The Psychic Aspects of Healing*

The Key to Being a Victim No More

"The greatest oak was once a little nut who held its ground."
—Author Unknown

MY NAME IS KATHLEEN O'Keefe-Kanavos and I am a woman on a mission to save lives and teach people how to become victims no more by living their lives to the fullest despite life's challenges.

There is almost always a point in the process of life where logic, reason, and medical expertise fail. At this point people often slip through the cracks, sometimes never recovering from dire situations. We forget that we hold the key to a victorious life rather than victims of policies, practices and unpredictable circumstances.

As a two-time breast cancer survivor whose cancer was missed both times by doctors and the tests on which they relied, I am determined to raise awareness about the importance of self advocacy, listening to our bodies, and trusting in our inner-guidance that often comes in the form of dreams. We can choose not to be a victim in life.

"Kathy, go home. You are healthy," my doctor told me again after my third mammogram, blood test and physical exam. I knew I had breast cancer. But my doctors would not listen to me. "Mammograms are our Gold Level Policy for finding cancer and you don't have it."

But that night my nightmares returned, told me again that I had breast cancer and to return the next day to my doctor, without a scheduled appointment. "You need exploratory surgery to find the cancerous spot." In the dream, my guide handed me a small white feather and said, "If you use this feather to verbally fence against your doctor's tests tomorrow, you will win and get the surgery you need. Believe," my guide said and stepped out of my dream.

My choice was to trust my nightmare or be a victim of misdiagnosis. What a decision! My doctor had undisputable medical tests from a leading cancer hospital in his "war chest." I had an imaginary feather from a dream in mine. My biggest challenge was who to believe, my doctor or my dream. And how to convince the one I did not believe that my choice was to be taken seriously. I believed in my guided dream and lived to write about it. Five years later I chose to self advocate and trust my dreams again rather than be a victim of hospital policy that was not in my favor. Against all odds, I survived stage-four cancer. The medical community had let me down twice. Yet, I chose to use my emotions of anger and fear to spur myself to action rather than allowing them to throw me into the defeated mentality of a victim.

The chance of my dreams finding cancer missed by "state of the art medical tests" *twice* was as lucky as winning the lottery two times in a row. Luck had little to do with it. Devine intervention did. Listen to your physician within. Don't tell your Higher Power how big your troubles are. She already knows. Tell your troubles how big your Higher Power is. Always work with your doctors, but never forget that you must make the final decisions, especially concerning life and death.

While undergoing months of chemotherapy, radiation treatment and surgery, I always carried jokes and affirmations in my pocket and read them aloud during challenging moments. This taught me to "laugh until it healed." Laughter raised my level of emotional vibration from low patient to high Thriver. I also learned to live by the rule, "Fake it 'til you make it." This is a form of role-playing. Role-playing is therapy often used by psychologists and psychiatrists. It is pretending which can change behaviors and emotions. This can be the first step toward becoming a survivor and ultimately a Thriver. Pretend to be happy until you truly are. Smile when you want to cry and you may find that you are filling with joy. Embrace your troubled emotions with inner-joy to help keep them balanced. That is a key to health.

Here are a few of my favorite affirmations and a joke that kept me balanced.

Affirmation

Loving myself heals my life. Healing my life heals my body.

Affirmation

I nourish my mind, body and spirit with dreams and meditations.

Joke:

A wife invited some people to dinner. At the table, she turned to their six-year-old daughter and said, "Would you like to say the blessing?"

"I wouldn't know what to say," the little girl replied.

"Just say what you hear Mommy say," the wife answered.

The daughter bowed her head and said, "Lord, why on earth did I invite all these people to dinner?"

You cannot be a victim without your permission. That permission can be given as active actions, verbal agreements or passive acquiescence through silence. Take responsibility for your actions. Dare to be the little nut that stands its ground to become a tall oak tree. Know your boundaries. Learn to say "Yes" to yourself by saying "No" to others. This is not being selfish. It is being responsible. If you do not take care of yourself before you take care of others, you will set yourself up for defeat by being an empty well trying to give nourishing water. Nourish yourself first.

Here are seven rules for becoming a victim no more:

1. Joy and sadness cannot share the same time and space because they are polar opposites. The same is true of victim and victor.

2. To be in pain is human. To suffer is a choice. Choose not to suffer.

3. View mistakes and difficult situations as opportunities to learn and you will never be victimized or defeated by challenges.

4. Victory is a state of mind as well as a state of being. So, set your mind to be victorious in all circumstances.

5. Respect your fears but don't let them rule your life. They remind you that you are alive. Let them guide you to make correct decisions.

6. Self advocate for the things you need in life and you will become a productive member of society and fulfilled human being.

7. Remember that you are never alone in your hour of need. We all have spiritual guides. We are their job and they take their job seriously.

Loving family members who have died are often given permission to help us by appearing in our dreams with messages of love, guidance and strength. We often forget that we are not human beings having a spiritual experience. We are spiritual beings having a human experience on the earth plane. Surviving trauma of any kind is part of the experience of life. Our spirit can connect with spiritual and Devine guidance though dreams, prayer and meditation. The dream realm is a way our spirit can phone home for help. Listen to your inner-guidance. Believe in the power of your dreams.

I am an advocate for organizations and movements based on encouraging women to stand up and be heard. Stories of women who listened to their female intuition and connected with their inner strength despite adversity, are empowering. They learned not to take "No." for an answer and they refused to be dismissed.

Be a squeaky wheel until you are heard. And remember to laugh in the face of challenges. It transforms you from victim to victor, takes away adversity's power and transfers that power to you. I have been cancer free for thirteen and eight years respectively. Yes, there is a wonderful life after any crisis.

We must balance our body and spirit with conventional and intuitive practices for complete health and wellness. Learning to embrace both is as easy as loving both. This in turn will give us the strength to rise above being a victim of circumstances to become an active participant in our journey through the follies of life.

In the words of the esteemed Golda Meir, "Trust yourself. Create the kind of self that you will be happy to live with all your life."

That is the key to being a victim no more.

 Kathleen O'Keefe-Kanavos is a two- time breast cancer survivor who penned *Surviving Traumaland: The Intuitive Aspects of Healing.* She is represented by Devra Jacobs DancingWordGroup Literary Agency & Steve Allen Media. She's a phone counselor for R.A. BLOCH Cancer Foundation, Q&A Cancer Columnist for *CapeWomenOnlineMagazine,* Radio Co-host *Beyond The 5 Senses,* an inspirational speaker, mentor, cancer volunteer, PATHEOS blogger, and part of LinkedIn's Wellness Authority. Kathy was born to a military family, raised in Europe, graduated from Munich American High School and Keene Teacher's College, taught Special Education and Psychology at University of South Florida.

https://www.facebook.com/pages/SURVIVING-CANCERLAND-The-Psychic-Aspects-of-Healing/142803307934

https://www.facebook.com/kathleen.o.kanavos http://www.youtube.com/user/kathyokeefekanavos http://www.survivingcancerland.com/ http://twitter.com/#!/PsychicHealing http://www.linkedin.com/profile/edit?trk=hb_tab_pro_top

http://www.myspace.com/video/vid/107692027

Web Site http://www.survivingcancerland.com/

Twitter- http://twitter.com/#!/PsychicHealing

PAGE II http://www.facebook.com/pages/SURVIVING-CANCERLAND-The-Psychic-Aspects-of-Healing/142803307934?ref=m

LinkedIn http://www.linkedin.com/profile/edit?trk=hb_tab_pro_top

Meet Patti Conklin a Vibrational Mediator

As a young child, I watched how people thought and spoke to each other. But word and thought rarely danced with the other, as they said one thing and meant another. Why did people do this? Didn't they know I could see what they meant? Of course, at such a young age, I didn't know they couldn't access this same information -- information that's clear as day to me, but muddled and clouded to them, and I was fascinated with how words and emotions were stored within each individual body.

Skip forward a few years, at the age of seven, to when I received what I considered to be my first visitation from "Father." I was told three things:

1. My greatest growth would occur between the ages of 38-42

2. My greatest contribution will be between 42 and 62

3. The purpose of my walk is to help people become
insubstantial without transitioning.

Throughout my life, I've learned that last phrase means to help people become unconditional without having to die for it. The following
pages are some of my beliefs, and reasons why I've come to the conclu-
sions of existence in how we react to each other and how we develop our
disease processes.

One portion of the bible that always made sense to me is: *In the
beginning first, there was the Word. The Word was God and the Word was
within God* ~ John chapter 1 verse 1.

Words didn't exist when the universe began. A cacophony of tones,
which we identify as frequency, echoed through the universe. At that
time, all souls existed in spirit form, outside of judgment and ego. So
how did we become this dense flesh?

As our souls evolved, we began to use words for communication
and emotion. We began to respond emotionally to our circumstances,
and eventually became less than unconditional beings. The words we use
to express judgment affected the ultra fast vibration of the spirit form
and, as the vibration slowed, spirits condensed into physical form, mark-
ing the beginning of humankind.

And the Word became flesh
—John chapter 1 verse 14.

All spoken, conditional words create a density, a slower moving
vibration within our subtle energy field, or as it's termed medically: the
immune system. They have a simple yet profound affect on everyone's
life, and there are no exceptions.

I've literally watched words form in the hemispheres of people's
brains, typically as a visual or auditory form of communication. These
words flow along a complex course through the individual's immune system, then store in individual cells. However, often what people think
and what they say don't match. An example of this is:

Thought: "Oh no, here comes Mark."
Voice: "Mark! It's so great to see you!"

Thus, two sets of conflicting words and emotions are stored in the body at the same time. I didn't know it then, but the *Word* became the most powerful cornerstone of my life's work. It's the most basic and important element in determining the course of our health and experience, and it remains the most significant way to observe which emotional memories are carried in our bodies.

Cellular Memory

We literally store a record of every word somewhere in our bodies. The subtle energy system (immune system) vibrates in a frequency unique to every human being. When words attach to emotions with a slower vibration, it is stored in the body, and the word creates a blockage.

Words with slow vibrations are created because of emotions that aren't unconditional, such as fear or anger, or when we exercise judgment towards another or ourselves. Each of these emotions is conditional in nature, and the blockages are so subtle that we don't notice until something exacerbates it. When an emotional memory is triggered, it gets our attention by manifesting as pain or illness.

Words that are neutral or nonjudgmental simply merge with the vibration of our bodies. These don't cause blockages, nor do they remove them, as even the most positive words can only preserve the status quo. Active vibration in the form of color or tone is the only way to clear blockages.

Energy flowing in the body is like the water in a creek. It runs at a certain rate in cubic feet per minute. If someone puts a log in the creek, the water dams up that area. The log isn't moving at the same rate as the creek, and the water must flow around it. A person might never notice the variation from a single log. However, if there is a heavy rain, then the increase rate of water could cause a flood. Then they wonder how everything became stopped up.

An ability to set and maintain healthy perceptions is the key to physical and emotional wellness. How you speak and feel is literally absorbed into your cells.

I had many typical childhood illnesses—earaches, mastoid colds, etc. Despite this, I maintained a very healthy, active life until my late 20s, when I developed both forms of Lupus. This was an incredibly challenging time. Lupus is a non-curable, non-treatable illness, and it's almost always fatal. My sons were little, and I was a single mom attempting to create a life for her children, working diligently in fund development work, but I was so sick I could barely get out of bed.

As the disease progressed, I experienced painful flare-ups in my joints, and my doctors strongly recommended high dosages of steroids. Some days I couldn't even move my joints because of stiffness. I watched myself in the mirror, and I would observe as welts rose on my face, and yellow ooze seeped out from those areas. My nervous system was so inflamed that simply putting clothes on was excruciatingly painful. The doctors advised me that, given the severity of both forms, I would possibly only live another 6-8 years.

I managed to cope daily as time went on, but I constantly questioned myself: Why, why did this happen to me? And so I thought, long and hard. I was very successful, I was a high school graduate, and I was working with individuals in fields who all had Ph.D.'s. There were doctors, doctors, and more doctors. Then it struck me, and I realized that I truly had an issue of self-worth. While I was very successful, I didn't feel worthy of my success, or indeed, qualified to do the type of work with which I was involved.

One night I had a dream, and in this dream God showed me how to move color within my body. In essence, the color was an active vibration that literally shook my lack of worthiness from each cell. My body cleared, and when I woke up I immediately sat down to meditate. I closed my eyes. I started breathing deeply, and I asked my body: What color do I need to remove my Lupus? I did this exercise for approximately 10 minutes, repeating it as I went through the course of my day, but I didn't feel any different. I still hurt. I was still weak. I still felt incredibly tired the next morning. I sat and thought about why God would show me colors and an exercise to do if it wasn't going to work? And then I realized my mistake.

The issue in my tissue was not Lupus. *It was self-worth.*

I needed to ask what color was required to increase myself self-worth. And so yet again, I sat quietly with my eyes closed, taking in deep breaths, relaxing my body completely and asking, "What color do I need to increase myself self-worth?" I waited, expecting vibrant colors—beautiful whites, sparkling greens, vibrant blues.

However, instead of seeing color, I heard a voice say, "Black."

Black?

What? Black is evil, it's dark -- all sorts of misperceptions and learned behavior flooded in. I realized that I needed frequency, not someone else's description of color. And so I simply trusted. I began to breathe in through my nose and imagined black coming in through the bottom of my feet up my body and out my mouth, just as God had shown me.

For me, personally, I didn't see my colors; I simply heard them as they changed and moved through my body. Again, I did this exercise for 10 minutes. Once finished, I began feeling lighter, with more mental clarity. The next day, I asked again, "What color do I need to increase my self-worth?" And this time I also asked, "What color do I need to remove my Lupus?" After 10 minutes of meditation, I was astounded with how wonderful I felt. From that day on, I didn't have another active period of Lupus. One year later, all of my blood work was normal. It has been almost 25 years, and I have not had a single symptom of Lupus. My blood work is checked yearly, and it continues to be clear.

The reason that color works is because color is an active vibration. There are two active vibrations on this planet: color and tone. All other vibrations, such as crystals, essential oils, Reiki, etc -- while they are incredibly important -- are passive vibration, which means that they don't have the frequency necessary to shake loose cellular memory from an individual cell. I've used my form of ColorWorks and ToneWorks now on over 100,000 people from around the world. It's amazing to work with someone, and within 10 minutes, have them feel more clear and out of pain. What a simple process for such dramatic results!

In the last 17 years, I have grown Healing Within, Inc into a successful international corporation, assisting thousands of people in understanding their behaviors, words and thoughts, in addition to helping them remove those blocked vibrations in their bodies using a specific technique I created known as Cellular Cleansing. Healing Within practitioners teach and lecture throughout the world on 'how' to become unconditional without having to die to achieve true happiness and health.

Patti Conklin is CEO and Founder of Healing Within, Inc,

Patti Conklin is a "Vibrational Mediator" with a rare vision. She identifies the core issues that form a disease process within the body. Intuitives, physicians, and people of every creed travel from each continent to broaden their view and participate in her compelling intuition, wellness and associate programs. Patti provides education, guidance, and certification in all of her unique and leading edge methods. Her insight is also highly sought after for professional conferences, seminars, workshops, and expos worldwide. She also extends her understanding of vibrational medicine, the science of energies, and yields to us how our actions and perceptions correlate with the ecology of our physical vessel. Patti empowers participants and inspires them toward the totality of wellness. Several authors have written about Patti's unique perception and sensitivity, and she is currently the Author of the 4 CD audio book set *Healing Within*. In the fall of 2012 Patti's long awaited book *God Within*, will be released.

https://www.facebook.com/PattiLConklin www.patticonklin.com
http://www.patticonklin.com,
https://www.facebook.com/PattiLConklin/info

Meet Betty Woodman of *Think it Real*

I DEVELOPED THE *Think It Real* program as a way to encourage creativity, vitality, and imagination. *Think It Real* promotes self-reflection about strengths, passions, and desires, as well as the doubts that keep us from our highest potential. This second aspect of the program is critical since disbelief often sabotages our efforts to "think it real."

A number of experiences inspired the creation of Think It Real, including work with bullying, dating violence, and leadership. I came to see that connections between these topics demonstrate the ways that far-reaching power relations of domination and conformity get in the way of creativity. I'll begin by describing the story of a young woman on the run from an ex-boyfriend. In some ways, her life was going well; she had recently graduated from college and accepted a job as an engineer. However, she was also trying to get away from a former boyfriend who was obsessed with her. She moved out of state to take the job, hoping that the distance would help her get away, but as is often the case, the point of break-up became the most dangerous. He threatened to kill her; he also threatened to kill specific family members. When he told her he had bought a gun, she moved again, got an unlisted phone number, and went to the police, who filed a warrant for his arrest if he came to the state looking for her. Previous experiences with restraining orders, however, had taught her that nothing would protect her if no one were there when he found her. So she also started the application process for a pistol permit. When he couldn't reach her at home on the phone, he began calling her on her work line, screaming obscenities. He finally threatened to come to her office building and find her. If anyone tried to stop him from getting to her and got shot in the process, he told her, it would be her fault because she wouldn't meet with him. She hung up the phone, walked into her manager's office, closed the door, and relayed the entire story of what had been happening. It was the first anyone at her workplace knew of the situation. She had been concerned that it would reflect poorly on her; others might judge her, question her competence, or look for some flaw that had allowed her to get into this situation. But at this point there was no other option; someone could get hurt. Workplace violence is real. We hear about case after case of a violent, controlling person coming after a partner at work. The good news is that this story has a happy ending. This happened over 20 years ago and that woman was me. I'm healthy and thriving, leading a life I love, teaching, learning, and growing.

But this isn't really about me at all. Sadly, this story is not unusual or rare. Violence against women is so common in our culture that we have become desensitized to daily reports of rape, violence, and murder. Statistics demonstrate that one in three women will experience violence in her lifetime; some believe the actual numbers are higher. Our popular culture sexualizes domination and violence against women and girls, putting forth sexual scripts that may limit sexual imagination and arousal patterns for men and women. Too often, though, we "other" this topic; it's critical to see how this affects men and boys as well as women and girls. In particular, it directly affects every boy or man who has been humiliated and shamed as a way to enforce a dominant form of masculinity. My interest may have been originally inspired by my desire to powerfully create my own life going forward but it is equally inspired by my recognition that this is *the* issue of our time. Until we understand this, we will not be able to diminish bullying, workplace violence, or dominant, toxic forms of leadership.

This point was made crystal clear a number of years later when I was a volunteer tutor for school-age boys living in foster group homes. During this time, I learned more about how toxic gender culture could be for boys as well as girls. I watched boys coping with distressing family realities while at the same time struggling to hold their own within a culture that humiliates and shames boys for any hint of vulnerability. I remember a young boy in particular; cigarette burns tattooed on his arms, his heart breaking from being ripped away from everything familiar, as well as the abuse he had suffered. A small boy, he became prey for school bullies. At the same time, I watched other boys in similar situations begin the process of "toughening up" as a survival strategy. This armoring, which also happens as the result of rigid childrearing or painful male gender socialization, itself leads to bullying behavior and dating violence. Bullies and batterers have often been bullied, shamed, or abused themselves. These pressures extend throughout the lifecycle. While working within predominantly male engineering organizations, I watched many men suffer within "pecking-orders" that promote the most macho and dominant men. This male hierarchy also values men according to class, race, and sexuality. Homophobia within many workplaces mirrors earlier school bullying; a significant amount of contemporary bullying is homophobic in nature.

These topics are related. When we pretend we are invulnerable or invincible, we swagger and strut: we lose sight of our power. We may pursue addictive desires for power as domination or conformity, which corrupt creativity. The fear of vulnerability is also entangled with desires for perfection, projected through body image, self-control, or addictions. By way of contrast, leadership and creativity depend upon the courage to embrace our vulnerability and need for each other as essential aspects of the human condition. Everyone is vulnerable. At the most fundamental level, we're mortal, we will die. During significant periods of our lives, we are dependent upon other people. We begin our life as babies and children. If we're lucky to live a long life, we wind up as elderly people who need help from others. Along the way, we may become ill, face adversity, or lose those we love. We turn to others or our communities for healing and comfort. The essential quality of the human condition is our universal vulnerability and our need for each other. Real courage, strength, and leadership come from embracing our vulnerability. Acceptance, humility, courage, and connection with others strengthen personal power. Power as creativity is life affirming, generative, and joyful.

Think It Real offers a process for anyone interested in awakening and strengthening personal power. The Think It Real program encourages self-reflection, "unlearning," and discovery. My workbook, *Think It Real: Awakening the Power Within* (fall 2012), details this process of cultivating freedom, power, and flourishing. A second workbook, *"Think It Real: Power, Creativity, and Relationship Dynamics,"* specifically addresses dynamics of controlling intimate, family, and bullying relationships. This upbeat, high-energy empowerment program dares us to imagine our most passionate desires and confront the fears that hold us back.

Think It Real bears the fingerprints of many. The process of thinking it real always happens together, with others. It begins with the wisps of an idea, which are infused with passion and strengthened by our relationships and communities. The intention for the Think It Real fan page is to provide a resource that encourages the self-reflection necessary for personal development and empowerment. We invite you to "think it real" and join our community on Facebook.

Betty J. Woodman, Ph.D., is principal of The Think It Real Company, Inc. Betty received her doctorate from Emory University (2012) in sustainability leadership, ethics, and education; previous degrees include philosophy and engineering. Betty's professional experiences include college teaching and executive management, as well as community engagement with domestic violence, foster group home, and transitional housing agencies. Betty develops innovative, high energy educational programs for college and high school students, offers personal development, business, and philosophical coaching, and speaks on topics ranging from domestic violence, bullying, and healthy relationships to sexual ethics, sustainability ethics, and sustainable leadership development.

Conclusion: It has been a pleasure

A universal love is not only psychologically possible; it is the only complete and final way in which we are able to love.
—Pierre Teilhard de Chardin

I MOST CERTAINLY HOPE that you all enjoyed being invited into the personal lives of these thirty incredibly inspiring faces behind the Pages of Facebook. I also hope that their stories brought you encouragement and even possibly piqued an interest in you to further explore and follow their Facebook Pages on a regular basis. Healing abounds there.

I found great joy in being able to share these handpicked, remarkable people with you. It is my hope that you all have garnished something wonderful from their positive attitudes. They are survivors in every sense of the word. Their *attitudes* — and how they have responded to life — have carried them through some very tough times. And that, my friend, is the definition of empowerment.

From my personal perspective, the reflection of our lives is *all about the attitude* with which we approach it. You know, as well as I do, that life isn't always easy and that there will always be a degree of challenge in our lives. It's a part of this human experience. However, you can choose to *respond* in any way that you desire — and that is a powerful thought, in and of itself.

What I have learned in the process of creating this book is that *givers always gain.* I was attracted *not* by the numbers of "likes" that my co-authors had, but by their *sincerity* to truly want to connect to their subscribers, from and through the heart. Frankly, it was their authentic interactions and lack of judgmental attitudes that attracted me to choosing them as my co-authors. And as you may know, I literally had thousands of pages to choose from.

By being willing to authentically share my own personal vulnerability in dealing with challenges, daily struggles and frustrations that life serves up — with my own subscribers on the "A Victim No More Facebook Page" — I learned firsthand that I was best able to get my subscribers' attention and help them to heal.

I showed them my pain, the steps that I took to deal with it. I also shared the feelings of happiness and inner peace that I experienced from using the tools that I teach in my book, for which the Page was created after. I found they were far more responsive when I did.

I also found a key to my own success by being multifaceted. By dropping the negative aspects of my ego, along with the need to prove myself to any other person, organization or anything outside myself, I truly was able to leave the victim mindset behind.

Let me be candid: I asked God/The Universe/the SOURCE of LOVE (whatever label you give the Creator of All That Is): "How can I best serve others for the highest good of all?" I have been doing this every morning — and I discovered that many of my co-authors have had the same routine.

When I do this, I know consciously that *I* am included in that blanketed request. I love myself and I am worthy of that. I embrace and accept that on every level. In fact, each morning in my quiet prayerful or meditative time, I ask for assistance throughout the day so that I can do my best to help others.

I often state: "Use me. Help me to do your work. Help me to be a vehicle of healing in order to assist others to break free from *suffering*." I also state: "Expand my ability to love and be loved — and expand my consciousness to hold that love."

I know the anguish of suffering. If you've read my book, *A Victim No More, How to Stop Being Taken Advantage Of*, you already realize this. When I observe people on my page sharing feelings and experiences that are causing them pain, my heart goes out to them. I do my best to reach out to them, as much as my schedule allows. I know that my co-authors have the same intentions. I've observed how committed they are to their Pages.

Anyone who knows me today is aware that I have a great sense of compassion and empathy for others who are still trapped in the cycle of the victim consciousness. I've made a conscious commitment in my life to help others learn how to step out of the line of fire — by refusing to be victimized.

Being the eternal "observer that I am by nature," I have watched and analyzed carefully the most shared posts within Inspirational Facebook Pages. I have viewed hundreds of Pages posts, day in and day out. I'd like to share with you what I have observed as the most well received messages in the inspirational sector of Facebook.

They include posts that talk about the following underlying messages:

- Changing your bad attitude into a positive one

- To value yourself

- Stop judging yourself and others

- Forgiving yourself and others

- Letting go of blame and shame

- Standing up for yourself and what you believe

- Leave your past behind you.

- Leave those people that aren't good for you, in your past

- What you believe is what you create

- Love yourself

- Love others

- Love and respect your children, animals, and the planet (environment).

- Find that love within yourself

- You have the right to equal rights, no matter your gender, age, or sexuality

- Live by the golden rule. (Do unto others, as you would like others to do unto you.)

- Stay in gratitude for it brings you more of what you are grateful for

- You are not defined by your past.

- Seek peace in all things

- Love more

Of course, there are more popular and inspiring messages, but these are the ones I have noticed that are shared most often. That told me people are hungry for this. People are craving love, honor, respect and a sense of dignity. They want to better themselves. And they want to be reminded of these action-oriented messages so they can integrate them into their lives.

In closing, I ask that you give yourself some credit. I bet that many of you have had similar experiences as our authors. I'm sure you have many stories to share. Well, Inspirational Pages on Facebook is where you can do that! *Take action* and share your story. Encourage your fellow subscribers. Comment. Like. Share. Pay it forward. Remember: *givers always gain.*

And that reminds me; I've already been seeking other unique and eclectic Page Admins who have new and different stories to tell about their lives. We have already scheduled a second edition of this book that will be coming out later this fall. And so — until next time . . . Namaste!

Lori Rekowski

Dear Readers,

In order to keep our authors work authentic and sincere. I have chose to include some unedited material to several of the stories. I hope that the beautiful messages touched your hearts and inspired you to know, that life is precious and in a moments notice can change on a dime. I encourage you to follow these remarkable teachers and their amazing wisdom by visiting their Facebook Pages. You most certainly will be blessed on many levels by their gifts of love and sharing for years to come.

About the Author

LORI REKOWSKI is a published Author, a professional Speaker, an Advocate for many nonprofit organizations and causes, and is a loving Mother and Grandmother. She has been a successful business entrepreneur and consultant for more than 25 years. She takes great pride in celebrating her healing process with others. In fact, she considers it her life purpose and passion.

A creative and analytical approach to her healing path during the past twenty years included research and participation in the holistic healing field. After years of seeking help from the traditional psychological health field, Lori was unsuccessful at maintaining long-term emotional stability. She knew (had faith) that there had to be a more effective way to emotional and spiritual stability. Lori found that the most effective assistance, allowing her own healing to accelerate, was the research and application of ancient healing modalities that are resurfacing in our society today, integrated with traditional medicine.

Lori studied hundreds of books, experienced private healing sessions and attended various seminars and classes throughout the United States, internationally, and on the Internet. She focused attention on her own unique inner connection to God and used the spiritual self-help field to heal successfully. This approach, and the use of these tools, accelerated her healing process at an amazing pace. She looks forward to teaching these tools to other survivors, assisting them in stepping into a healthy and happy lifestyle.

http://www.facebook.com/avictimnomore
https://www.facebook.com/TheFacesBehindThePagesThatInspire
http://www.pagesthatinspire.com/
https://www.facebook.com/pages/A-Course-in-Courage-Victory-Tour/128303377311139
http://www.avictimnomore.com

14263345R00118

Made in the USA
Charleston, SC
31 August 2012